# Rational
# Thinking

# Rational

# Thinking

## A Study in Basic Logic

John B. Bennett

Nelson-Hall ⊞ Chicago

Library of Congress Cataloging in Publication Data

Bennett, John Boyce, 1911-
   Rational thinking.

  Includes index.
    1. Logic. 2. Fallacies (Logic) 3. Inference
(Logic) I. Title.
BC108.B42     160      79-17555
ISBN  0-88229-285-4  (cloth)
ISBN  0-88229-739-2  (paper)

Manufactured in the United States of America

10 9 8 7 6 5 4 3 2 1

# Contents

# Introduction

Man, especially western man, is smugly confident about his capacity for rational thought. His assurance that he is gifted at sound thinking is revealed by the way he punctuates his conversation with claims to rationality. "Any reasonable person will agree with me that. . . ." "Now let us get our facts together and line them up." "Since what I have said so far cannot be challenged, we are forced to conclude. . . ." "This is only common sense."

If we are all endowed with a singular gift of reasoning, why is it we are not all healthy, wealthy, and wise? Why does our economic system often go awry? Why are there different economic systems at all? Why does our political system have within it sharply differing positions? Why do we fall out with each other? Why do we sometimes fall out with ourselves? Why do we find such confusion in so many quarters?

One answer to these questions lies in our failure to follow a few simple rules for sound thinking. This is not to say that fallacious reasoning is the sole source of our many woes. It is certainly not the only matter involved where political, economic, theological or other ideologies clash. Sharp differences in these areas stem from the different premises or presuppositions upon which the systems of thought are based. When premises or presuppositions are radically different no amount of reasoning can be expected to bring results that coincide. In fact, the strict application of logical principles may widen divisions.

A dialectical materialist, for example, a Marxian communist, works with presuppositions that are enormously different from the presuppositions of free enterprise capitalists. If the adherents of these respective systems followed the same patterns of reasoning, their conclusions would still be very different. A theologian who believes in the literal interpretation of the scriptures could conceivably use a system of reasoning like that characteristic of a critical or rationalistic student of the scriptures. But, since their undergirding presuppositions are very different, their final pronouncements in theology would be very different.

Since dialectical materialists differ among themselves, free enterprise advocates differ among themselves, Biblical literalists, rationalists, and so on, differ among themselves within their respective areas of commitment, we suspect that tracks in reasoning have somehow veered away from each other. This may be the result of the curious situation we face in the fact that there are many more ways to go astray in reasoning than there are straight and narrow paths to tread in sound thinking.

For one thing, there are more than three dozen ways to misuse or abuse single propositions. Only about half a dozen rules are needed as guidelines for stating single propositions properly. And then again, when we start putting two or more propositions together in order to reach a proposition we can state as a conclusion, the number of possible errors is fairly staggering. There are more than two hundred and fifty ways to arrange two propositions and a conclusion with the hope of drawing the conclusion from the premises. But, only a couple of dozen of these are valid. On the one hand, then, it would seem to be that we are faced with a hopeless situation when the odds against our being correct in any simple three-proposition argument are at least ten to one.

On the other hand, there are so few simple, easily mastered rules for right reasoning—certainly as these rules apply to our everyday lives—that we should be able to improve our thinking processes enormously. More details will be given in certain later chapters about this situation.

Meanwhile, just what is logic as an elementary, basic study all about? The word logic derives from a Greek word *logos* which has quite a bit of meaning packed into its two syllables. *Logos* implied to Greek philosophers (and implies to us) that there is a rational, orderly principle in the universe itself. It also implies that words must be clear and used in an orderly way if propositions accepted as *true* are to be related in a *valid* manner so as to yield *reliable*, and hence *true*, conclusions. This is what we often refer to as sound thinking.

The *-logy* part of a number of English words derives from *logos*. "Biology" is the study of and reasoning about *bios* or life. "Geology" is the study of and reasoning about the *gaia* (or *ge*), or the earth. "Psychology" is the study of and reasoning about the *psyche*, or soul or mind. "Epistemology" is the study of and reasoning about *episteme*, or knowledge itself, a careful analysis of how we know, what we know. This list, too long for completion here, includes "ontology," the study of the nature of reality; "axiology," the study of values; "petrology," the study of rocks; "neurology," the study of the nervous system; "herpetology," the study of reptiles; "arachnology," the study of spiders; etc. A longer list would also include some instances in which logic as an incorporated concept seems to some to have been abused, as, for example, in "astrology" and "phrenology."

Interest in a serious study of logic is currently on the upswing. This interest has become so widespread that of the making of logic books—good ones at that—there appears to be no end. Why, then, another? This volume presents the following features not found in combination in other texts on logic.

1.  The basic elements of logic are presented in a form suitable for an intensive three-quarter-hour, lower level college or university course, or a more leisurely three-semester-hour course in logic. Relatively few extant publications in this area can be satisfactorily developed within a quarter or a semester.

2.  The principles of logic applicable to daily living are presented in simple form, free from all but essential technical terminology. A discussion of all exercises is included, so that a diligent person can teach himself elementary logic. Many texts move so quickly into symbolic logic that they discourage the beginning student. Some devote a great deal of space to topics of a special nature such as probability and statistics, for example, which are important and useful, but which require book-length treatment for those who need to use probability and statistics with facility. Still other works devote a good deal of space to topics which belong more properly in psychology or epistemology. Logic is, of course, so closely linked to these fields that a complete separation is not feasible, but overlapping is reduced to a minimum in these pages.

3.  Illustrative materials have been selected for their

timeliness and practical appeal to the wide range of student types now encountered in the nation's burgeoning continuing education and extension courses, including teachers furthering their study, secretaries, nurses, businessmen, and hardhats. Many logic books, whatever their technical merit, devote an inordinate amount of space to cute, game type exercises and illustrations. Some authors enjoy the sort of tricky lines of "reasoning" that lead circuitously from the proposition "All koala bears love their children" to "All koala bears abuse their children." Some are fond of non-oboe-playing alligators. Some invite us to play around with brain teasers: at what point will two microbes that multiply every minute fill a test tube half full? What is the smallest number of queens that can be placed on a chess board so as to command all squares? The study of logic leads into enough amusing encounters to keep us entertained without our having to manufacture unimportant puzzles.

4. The appendix includes techniques which enable visually handicapped, and even totally blind students to learn logic at a pace equalling that of students with normal vision. In fact, this work, in its initial form, grew out of a situation in which the author encountered blind students in his regular class in logic.

There are four areas of emphasis in the study of logic. First, there is the consideration of linguistic usage and fallacies associated with words and sentences as such. These are called "informal" or "material" fallacies where meanings may be obscure or, if seemingly clear, actually misleading or lacking in supportive evidence.

Second, there is the study of inference. That is, given one proposition whose meaning is clear, or a set of propositions whose meanings are clear, what may be inferred therefrom? What conclusions may be drawn from them?

Third, there is the application of logic in the sciences, both natural and social: probability, statistics, the scientific method, and inductive reasoning.

Fourth, there is modern, or symbolic, logic which is based upon the fact that classical, traditional logic is incomplete, and which has extended the systematizing of logic into a rigorous mathematical form. This type of logic is important for philosophers and scientists, but it is not the kind of logic we use in ordinary pursuits.

This work will cover the first two areas since they are of most immediate concern to and use for all of us. Part 1 will be an analysis of linguistic, or informal, or material fallacies. Part 2 will be an analysis of inferences from single propositions and of syllogistic reasoning, the deduction of a conclusion from related propositions.

Footnotes and references have been virtually eliminated, because direct dependence upon other sources has been studiously avoided. In an established area like logic, one must, of course, present generally accepted principles available in many basic books.

The editors of several periodical publications graciously offered blanket permission to use direct quotations from their pages for illustrations and exercises, provided only that credit to specific sources be given. But it seemed unfair, or at least inappropriate, to identify the source of a fallacy without balancing the account with some illustration of proper applications of logic from the same source. Such an undertaking would enlarge the book greatly, and, after all, it is with fallacies that we are primarily concerned.

Illustrative materials, therefore, have been suggested by editorials, letters to editors, essays, political speeches, advertisements and personal encounters. But, the illustrations and exercises are rendered, within the limits of the author's imagination, in fictional form. Some of them, however, cannot be completely disguised without weakening one intent of the book: to alert the student to the extent to which we are clouded about with abuses of logic, sometimes deliberate and sometimes inadvertent.

Those already acquainted with basic logic may note a few instances of originality in simplified techniques of notation and graphic illustrations of the principles of logic in ways that both sighted and visually handicapped students have found to be efficient and helpful.

Specific credit is due the following, but each is absolved of any responsibility for any points of weakness in the work:

Dr. Carroll S. Feagins, head of the Department of Philosophy at Guilford College, who some decades ago introduced the author to logic as an area of study which he had missed in college.

Dr. Maurice B. Morrill, and the Western Carolina University Committee on Research of which he was chairman, for a grant which supported the research and experimentation involved in that part of the work relevant to the visually handicapped.

Ms. Georgia Hickes, a braillist, who, in initial conferences, perceptively delineated procedures for research and experimentation which proved fruitful.

Students in logic classes who used the text in mimeographed form over a two-year period, occasionally noting inconsistencies or obscurities, and blind students from the "Early Bird Program," conducted each summer by Professor Minor Wilson and Mr. David Waldrop, who made valuable suggestions about points of special concern to them.

Professor Donald Walhout, Rockford College philosopher, and Dean Richard E. Hutcheson of State University College, Potsdam, both braillists and versed in logic, who examined portions of the text particularly pertinent to working with the blind, reassured the author by their commendation of techniques used, and added valuable suggestions of their own which have been incorporated into the appendix.

Dr. John E. Loftis, III, of the English faculty at the University of Northern Colorado, and Dr. Michael P. Jones, colleague in philosophy at Western Carolina University, whose criticisms were directed toward syntax, accuracy, and clarity.

My wife, who, for four decades, has graciously refrained from flaunting the superior nature of intuitive feminine logic and, more recently, has been tolerant of dislocations in family pursuits during the elephantine gestation and labor period that being "with book" has required.

# Part 1:

# Material or Informal Fallacies

Logicians have arrived at no common agreement as to the naming of material or informal fallacies or as to an organization for their presentation. This section will include some three dozen fallacies with some but by no means all of the various terms logicians use for those fallacies. As the table of contents clearly shows, there is an imbalance as to the number of fallacies falling within the various groups and an imbalance as to the space devoted to various fallacies. It is simply the case that some types of fallacy include more sub-types than other types do and some kinds of fallacies are encountered much more frequently and in more varied forms than others.

Occasionally, an illustration may be used in more than one section of the book, for some illustrations represent more than one type of fallacy. Some technical terminology is convenient and perhaps necessary, and the technical terms are easy to define, easy to illustrate and therefore

rather easy to remember. The important purpose of the
study, however, is to learn to spot fallacies in reasoning in
political speeches, in editorials, in advertisements, and in
a variety of situations where arguments are being advanced.

Indeed, we should be cautious about academic jargon.
One may find his position in a discussion weakened if he
uses technical terminology. Suppose someone responds to
an argument that has been advanced, "That's a good example of *petitio principii.*" He is not likely helping himself to be persuasive. His friend in conversation may be
mystified, embarrassed, or even irritated by a seeming
evasion. However, if one uses, in lieu of "That's a good
example of *petitio principii,*" "You are begging the question," he may still be risking a bit of offensive effrontery.
It might be better to ask politely, "Please drag that by
again. Are you sure you haven't implied your conclusion
in the reasons you are giving to start with?"

Or suppose one responds in a discussion with, "Now
don't try to pull that *argumentum ad hominem* stuff on
me." Unless his friend is versed in logic he is guilty of one
of the very fallacies discussed in this section—the fallacy
of obscuration, burying a thought behind verbiage.

In any case, an argument or discussion is more appropriately approached by reasoned discussion than by pres-
tigious labels for ideas. Logic is for use, not ostentatious
display. This is not to say that no good purpose is served by
enlarging one's vocabulary through any form of significant
study. It is rather to caution that in expressing to others
what one has learned technically, it is more gracious and
courteous, and thus more effective in the art of practical
persuasion, if one simplifies without talking down to another.

# Chapter 1

# Linguistic Fallacies

With his remarkable tool of language man can accumulate the wisdom—and the foolishness—of the ages. Through his reasoning capacity man can sort out the two, separating the wisdom from the foolishness.

Reasoning and language are so interrelated that canons for their proper usage must be established and observed. Much mischief can result from the improper or unclear use of language itself. This may well be the meaning of the story in Genesis of the thwarted attempt to build the Tower of Babel. It has been said, "Whom the gods would destroy, they first make mad." It might be added, "And whom the gods would make mad they first confuse in their communication." Inability to communicate with others is frustrating. Inability to communicate with one's self is madness.

Our first chapter, then, deals with one of the kinds of problems encountered in attempts to think and communicate with clarity, that of linguistic usage. The importance of such an analysis is pointed up in situations like the following.

In the course of a congressional hearing a senator became angry when an economist termed communism "monolithic." The economist insisted he was condemning, not commending, communism by the use of the term. Another legislator claimed that he was not filibustering but only insisting that a certain proposed bill be given due deliberation.

A lawyer impressed a jury to the disadvantage of a defendant by asking the defendant, "Oh, you *say* you did not know the plaintiff very well, do you?"

A man who holds the opinion that all conservatives are wealthy met an obviously wealthy man at a cocktail party. He later said to a friend, "That fellow must surely be a conservative."

Each one of these items involves one of the types of linguistic fallacy examined in this chapter. The dispute between the senator and the economist involves a form of equivocation termed simple ambiguity. They should be able to resolve their difference by agreeing upon a clear meaning of the word "monolithic." In the courtroom scene the lawyer is using emphasis or accent to imply the defendant is not really being truthful. The observer of the relationship between conservative and wealthy people has committed an error in converting a proposition, changing the positions of subject and predicate without qualifying the new subject with the word "some." We now proceed with further discussion of these and other fallacies.

## 1. Equivocation

The term "equivocation" literally means "equal speak," and is the speaking or writing of a word or sentence which can have two or more meanings without the speaker or the writer making clear which specific meaning is intended. Equivocation takes two forms, simple ambiguity and amphiboly.

a. *Simple Ambiguity*

When a word has two or more meanings it is said to be ambiguous. Many words in the English language have two or more meanings and thus aid and abet in the matter of equivocation.

Suppose someone says, "It is hard to think right and harder to do right." Does "think right" mean "think correctly in a logical sense?" Or does it mean "follow Buddha's injunction to 'right thoughts,' " presumably "good" or "worthy" thoughts? Is "do right" a matter of ethical conduct or is it the efficient practice of scientific procedures? The meaning of "right" in these cases is not at all clear.

Debates grow quite warm over whether "right to work" legislation promotes "rights" of individuals. When prices are stated under a "fair trade" listing, questions arise as to what is fair to whom. When someone says that the taking of property is thievery and that the government in levying taxes is taking property and therefore engaging in thievery, he is being very careless with the meanings of the words "taking property" and "thievery."

Of less significance, at least for the layman if not for philosophers influenced by George Berkeley, are questions which sometimes arouse heated argument. Ask a group, "If a tree falls in an uninhabited forest does it make any sound?" and you will get fervent "yes" and "no" responses. Obviously, however, if participants in the discussion can agree upon the meaning of the word "sound" they can resolve their differences. If "sound" is defined in psychological and physiological terms as requiring a biological receptor to carry impulses to the brain and no inhabitants

—again psychologically and physiologically speaking—are present, there can be no sound. On the other hand, if one defines "sound" as a physicist would as the setting up of waves in some medium like air, dust, or an electrical recording device, then there is sound.

Puns are perhaps the most frequently encountered forms of equivocation. Two friends were engaged in a serious analysis, but from different perspectives, of the involvement of the United States in Vietnam. One began a statement about something he could not understand in the other's position with the words, "I cannot conceive . . ." But he was interrupted before he could state what he found inconceivable by, "I know you cannot conceive! You are a male!" This, by the way, also illustrates the fallacy of "misuse of humor" that will be discussed in a later chapter, for lines of thought were irreparably disrupted. The punster, proud of his sally, laughed down serious efforts to resume the conversation.

A staff counselor of a youth organization approached a young man during a week-end workshop to ask about the progress of a project on which the young man had been working the evening before. He inquired, innocently, "How did you make out last night?" The gales of laughter from others overhearing the question puzzled him until he was informed that "make out" has to do with romantic accomplishments and not, as he had thought, with the success of any particular undertaking. The over-thirty person finds he must keep informed about many changes in word meanings. For example, he used to be complimented by being described as "square." Not so any longer! He had best not use "gay" to describe a party of the night before. "Monkey," "bird," "box," and many other erstwhile commonplace words that it might not be entirely in good taste to list have taken on meanings not in earlier dictionaries.

Some of our most frequently used words have taken on a number of accepted and quite different meanings over the years. Without consulting a dictionary one can come up in five minutes with a dozen different meanings of the word "good." "That was a good deed," is an ethical judgment. "He is a good plumber," means he is competent in his vocation but the statement says nothing about his ethics. A simply spoken "Good!" can mean "that's enough," or "I agree with you." "Good" can mean a considerable amount, as, "That's a good catch of fish," or "I had to wait a good while for him." "Good" can mean tasty, as, "That's good coffee." "Good" can express commendation, as, "Good boy!" Or it can express condemnation, as, "Good for him!"

Some dictionaries shortchange the common word "is." They merely give a line or two like this: "The third person singular, present indicative of the verb to be, as, 'It is a dog.' " But "is" can assert predication, as, "Music is a healing force." "Is" can express class inclusion, as, "The task of the president is difficult" meaning that the task of the president is included in difficult tasks. "Is" can assert other relationships, such as equivalence, implication, and identity.

Ambiguity can also arise from similarities in sounds two words may have. One illustration derives from the legendary report that "Apollo entertained Venus on Mount Olympus where he fed her ambrosia and nectar." "Necked her" is, of course, a dated term for a mild form of "making out." "A bun is the lowest form of wheat" is a strained pun on the claim that "a pun is the lowest form of wit," which has something to do, no doubt, with the fact that the better (or is it worse?) the pun, the more audible the groans of the listeners.

Not all equivocal or ambiguous words are to be spurned.

While we risk complicating our language unduly, some assertions which blend meanings are appropriately expressive. Here are a couple of many possible illustrations. It is generally agreed that man is biologically an animal. So when we observe someone doing something unworthy and selfish or perhaps being somewhat overly indulgent we may be tempted to say, "He's acting like an animal." But we soften the expression by saying, "Well, he's only human." So we do not intend to eliminate all of our figurative language.

When a committee promoting the building of a new hospital wing uses the slogan, "Be a Brick—Buy a Brick," let us not quibble. Let us be a brick and buy a brick. Nor should we be inclined to reject, "She's a real doll," or "He's a square shooter," or a thousand and one other relatively poetic phrases. Equivocation as a fallacy is a matter of serious concern when there is a deliberate attempt to confuse issues or mislead a reader or listener.

### b. *Amphiboly*

When a sentence, not just a word, has more than one possible meaning, it may be because the words have been "thrown around" carelessly, because, that is, the sentence is *amphibolous*. The "amphi-" part of the word means "around" or "two ways" or "two sides," as in amphibious or amphitheater. The "-boly" or "-bolous" part of the word derives from the Greek word *ballo,* meaning I throw, from which we very possibly get the word "ball."

Amphibolies are usually created by sloppy or incorrect grammar or by ignoring simple rules of syntax. One such rule that is often ignored results in a misplaced modifier. The principle in English is normally that a word or phrase modifies the closest noun to which it can apply. Well-worn but clear illustrations of amphiboly resulting from breaching this principle are want ads like the following. "For Sale: Grand piano by a woman with ornate legs." "For Sale: House by a man with a big bay window."

Sometimes subject and predicate are shifted for rhetorical effect. But such a switch should not be made if vagueness is the possible result. The Delphic oracle was gifted at amphibolous replies to questioners, for she seems not to have given answers to questions just for rhetorical effect. Asked to predict the outcome of a battle, the oracle replied, "The Greeks the Persians shall subdue." Now just who is going to subdue whom? Only better syntax can clear this up: "The Greeks shall subdue the Persians" or "The Persians shall subdue the Greeks," depending upon what is meant.

Asked to identify the wisest man, the oracle reported, "No man is wiser than Socrates." But does this identify Socrates as the wisest of men? No. It only states that Socrates is as wise as an indefinite, possibly large, number of men who may be wiser than the general populace. To be sure, the interpretation frequently given this story is that Socrates was the single wisest man for he has added to his sum of wisdom the knowledge that he has some limitations to his wisdom. Socrates, according to this view, had added self-knowledge to the wisdom he already possessed while other wise men had not. But the fact that philosophers still debate this point indicates that the oracle's statement is not crystal clear.

Numerous irregular sentences, many of which are amphibolous, must be restated in strict logical form when we examine syllogistic reasoning later. For example, "All men are not wise" must certainly mean, "Some men are not wise"—or in even stricter logical form, "Some men are excluded from the wise." We do not mean by the expression, "All men are not wise" that "All men are to be excluded from the wise." "All that glitters is not gold" must mean that some things that glitter are not gold rather than that all things that glitter are excluded from golden things. The problem of irregular or vague propositions is so important that a chapter will be devoted to this topic later.

Many instances of amphiboly are trivial or merely humorous. But some call for clarification. One such instance has to do with a consideration of some aspects of cloning —the production of offspring genetically identical with a parent. A research physiologist was reported as saying that in cloning one may "produce organisms resistant to all known antibiotics or cancer forming bacteria." Did he mean organisms resistant to cancer forming bacteria or did he mean that cancer forming bacteria may be produced? It might possibly be that organisms resistant to cancer forming bacteria could be useful in preventing or treating cancer—and therefore desirable to produce. But cancer forming bacteria produced by cloning, or bacteria that generate cancer producing substances so produced, would be a different matter.

A check on the original source corrected the amphiboly-produced ambiguity about cloning. The original statement was that in cloning one might "produce organisms resistant to all known antibiotics or to cancer forming bacteria." The second "to" had been omitted. Either combination of results would be a mixed blessing of course.

Lawyers, legislators and indeed all of those who must prepare technical reports and documents must be very alert to amphibolous statements. Wills, for example, must make it clear whether a sum of money is bequeathed to each of, say, two or more children to share, or whether a specific sum goes to each. A will would almost certainly be the subject of litigation if it were to read, "I do hereby bequeath, give and assign to my three children, Thomas Bledsoe, Richard Bledsoe, and Harry Bledsoe, the sum of $90,000." Did the will intend that each of the Bledsoes should receive $30,000 or that each should receive $90,000?

To engage in clear thinking and communication one must define words with care and in such a way that speaker and listener, or writer and reader clearly agree upon their meanings. And then he must arrange the words so that the syntax is such that the words will convey a single clear meaning. Mathematicians have devised syntactical rules that relieve mathematical propositions of equivocation. Suppose someone says orally, "Three times four plus eight is twenty." Someone might challenge the statement. "No, not at all," one might say. "Three times four plus eight is thirty-six." The expression can be clarified by enclosing the three times four in parentheses if the first speaker's figure of twenty is intended or enclosing the four plus eight in parentheses if the second speakers figure of thirty-six is intended. Word users would do well to emulate mathematicians in punctuating when writing or in inflection when speaking to attain clarity.

## 2. EUPHEMISMS

"Euphemism" derives from the Greek *eu,* meaning well or good, and *phemizein,* meaning to speak. If the etymological meaning of euphemism and its present use were the same, it would not be listed among fallacies in logic. But, the term has come to apply to the use of pleasant and appealing words to replace unpleasant but more accurately descriptive words. Euphemizing might well be considered in the study of psychology, for it is a form of resorting to word magic as a psychological ploy. We try to soften the dread meaning of death by using "passed away," "gone away," or "made his demise."

Educators are quite gifted at the use of euphemistic language. Sometimes they decline to admit that they reject any students who apply for admission to their institutions by saying, "Two hundred seventy students selected themselves out of our program." What they mean, of course is, "We rejected 270 student applications." Registrars and deans much prefer "attrition rate" to "failure rate" or "flunk-out rate."

Registrars and deans, by the way, have been euphemistically upgraded in many situations. Registrars have become "vice-chancellors in charge of records." Deans have become "vice-chancellors for academic affairs." College and university presidents cannot slighted, naturally, and so they have become "chancellors." The only discernible change in these various posts otherwise is usually an increase in salary and perhaps additional administrative and clerical assistance.

For an institution of higher learning to pay an athlete for his performance is an abhorrent notion. So sports pages do not include any mention of so mercenary an idea. Instead they display pictures of athletes posing with members of their families and with college representatives as they sign an agreement to an "athletic grant" and sometimes even an agreement entitled, in seemingly inherently contradictory wording, an "athletic scholarship." Educational institutions do not have salesmen, promoters, or money-raisers. Instead they have offices of public relations, or offices of institutional research and development.

A state budget commission revealed that its members had been apt students in such institutions. When the state highway commission passed on to the budget commission its report on unsafe bridges in the state, the budget commission softened the report considerably. The budget commission listed some bridges as "needing widening or

resurfacing to eliminate only moderately hazardous situations," some as "structurally deficient" and others as
"structurally obsolescent."

Military spokesmen are among those who are very
gifted at euphemistic language. In the throes of retreating
before an advancing enemy during the 1970s conflict in
southeast Asia, South Vietnamese military officers said,
"We have not abandoned any territory. We have merely
withdrawn troops because of certain tactical demands."
Such language harks back at least to the 1940s when the
late Chiang Kai-shek interpreted a similar series of defeats
as being "strategic retreats." Military strategists do not
step up the pace of war, increase bombing, or anything
so crass and cruel. They "escalate" various maneuvers.
They do not attack supply or troop movement routes. They
engage in "interdiction of the opposing forces."

One of the more remarkable instances of euphemizing
came about directly after World War II. Some political
figure ventured the proposal that the United States use
military force to reduce Russia to impotence. Immediately
the question was put, "Do you mean to advocate attacking
Russia? Starting a war?" "Oh no," he replied. "We won't
be starting any war. We will only be engaging in anticipa-
tory retaliation. We know one day Russia is going to strike
at us. So we merely retaliate now for what we know is coming later." It is probably a good thing for civilization that
this remarkable bit of euphemistic phrasing was not widely
persuasive.

### 3. Obscuration

If a house obscured by trees can be found by following
directions, there is a house there. It simply cannot at first
be seen or cannot be seen clearly, because it is hidden or
partially hidden. When a proposition is expressed in words

that are vague, copious, uncommon or polysyllabic, or
(sometimes) all of these, the idea back of the proposition is
hidden, or obscured. In some instances, unlike the house
and the trees, there may even be no idea for one to discover.

Medical doctors probably do not engage themselves in
obscuration as much as jokesters would have it. But if
your physician were to say, "You have circumorbital hae-
matoma," he would be giving a technical name for a black
eye in rather obscure wording. Or a doctor might tell you
that you have a "virally produced cellular excrescence
which has resulted in a dermal protuberance." That is,
"You have a wart." A doctor or a physiologist engaged in
research might know immediately what "deep hypothermic
circulatory reduction" means, but a layman can understand more readily the simple phrase "body chilling."

On the other hand, one might be pleased if a doctor
combined euphemistic wording and obscuration by recording in his medical report, "Diagnosis: Enterobius vermi-
cularis. Prescription: Gentian Violet as an anthelmintic."
This sounds somewhat more pleasant—or at least less
unpleasant— than a notation reading, "This patient has pin-
worms and I have prescribed worm medicine." A doctor
may, of course, be impressed with the utility of placebos
and hand you a prescription, this time in legible script,
reading, "Ten grains monoacetylsalicylic acid, three times
daily." You will be getting aspirin, of course.

Advertisers use a form of obscuration, sometimes termed
"prestige jargon," as, for example, a description of some
over-the-counter capsules as containing "ergocalciferol,
riboflavin, pyroxidine hydrochloride, and cobalamin, all
of which are aids in maintaining good health." These
words may be clear and meaningful to medical doctors,
pharmacists and nutritionists. But such an advertisement

is more likely directed toward the general public, for which the words, however impressive, are meaningless, than toward a special group of professional personnel.

The military mind is as apt at producing obscure language as it is euphemistic language. The Navy Department spent some several hundred thousand dollars for research on the "aerodynamic analysis of the unpowered, airsupported, rotating flare." The purpose of the research was to learn if circular, plastic discs, similar to the toy Frisbee or Pluto Platter, were useful as flare carriers. At last report the findings seem to have been fully disappointing.

Again, educators must be noted as among the sinners against the principles of logic in their use of obscure language. A representative of an educational foundation said to a group of college officials:

> It might well be anticipated on your part that the board of directors of the foundation will be inclined to view your application in a more sanguine manner if in generating your proposal you will avoid abstractions, and exercise ingenuity in eliminating duplicatory items in your conspectus.

All he meant was: "Your application will make a better impression if it is concrete and original."

A state board of education approved a half million dollar grant with the following interpretation:

> The purpose of this project is to develop the capability for institutions of higher learning and community agencies and organizations to coalesce for the development of community services and create a model for the coordination of such services that would maximize some of the available resources from a number of institutions and provide communication and priority needs and the response of the educational needs of a given community.

After several readings it appears somewhat plausible to say that the purpose of the grant was "to get community agencies to cooperate in developing resources for education."

Those listening to a social scientist involved in economic analysis might be exposed to the following:

> Let me review by way of summary what I have been presenting to you. If there is a latent tendency in a substantial number of individuated subjects to indicate a proclivity toward accumulating an exorbitant proportion of profit marginal shares of a given stock then unless such attitudinal inclinations can be subordinated to a socially conscious altruism a dislocation in a specified area may be anticipated.

What he means is that if selfish individuals persist in trying to corner parts of the market, they cause economic problems.

The following advertisement might be understandable to someone experienced in electronics or very familiar with sound equipment, but it communicates little to an ordinary shopper out to find good amplifying equipment at a reasonable price:

> The Stoa Model VI power operating amplifier is an incredible piece of equipment that uses multiple-site epitaxial output devices, resulting in a phenomenal power bandwidth and tremendous current and thermal capability. It has the world's finest hysteresis synchronous motor.

Most shoppers would need a translation of such a paean of praise.

Read the following carefully:

> This hyperbolic status index is at one and the same time an evaluative communication matrix and a reciprocal

sociometric gradient. The attribution of intuitive communication via a centralized coalition of role structure will prove through the use of the index to be interpersonally negative unless there is a functionally interdependent role equilibrium.

If you discerned anything meaningful in the preceding two sentences it is by remarkable coincidence. They were concocted from a collection of words selected somewhat at random but sounding as if they come from some area of behavioral science. The point is to illustrate how quite useful words may be arranged to express no idea at all.

Strictly speaking, obscuration can be faulted in terms of principles of logic when it involves deliberately covering information with verbiage. At the same time, clarity is usually a virtue. If one does not care to communicate clearly, why bother to communicate at all?

Dictionaries have come a long way in clarifying words so as to aid us in our attempts to be clear in communication. The eminent lexicographer Dr. Samuel Johnson presented a good many definitions in obscure wording. He defined a network thus: "Anything reticulated or decussated at equal distances, with interstices between the intersections." A current Webster's dictionary gives the definition as: "An arrangement of fibers, threads, cords, wires, or such, crossing and fastened at fairly regular intervals so as to leave open spaces between them." This by no means covers all of our uses of the word "network," but it defines quite well the basic form of the word from which other uses—a radio network or television network, for example—stem. Dr. Johnson defined the word "dross" as "The recrement or despumation of metals." Compare this with a modern definition: "A scum of waste matter formed on the surface of molten metal."

## 4. ACCENT, OR LIFTING OUT OF CONTEXT

The fallacy of accent, and its dramatic form, lifting out of context, occurs when someone by emphasis—italics, full capitals, position in printed columns, or otherwise—stresses a point so that it gets considerably more notice than unstressed but important words or phrases.

A columnist writing on a political matter begins, "This will necessarily be a long column, so if you can't finish it or must finish it hastily, all right. But let me stress first of all, so that you will remember, that Senator Soundoff is proposing a dangerous piece of legislation." In anticipating criticism from careful readers the columnist may mention casually and very briefly some counter arguments. But for many readers he has already been persuasive in his forceful language and in the favorable positioning of his criticism. He has accented his own point of view.

Advertisers often use the accenting device of lifting from context. A form this takes is the case of an advertisement quoting from a review of a television program: "The most watchable rerun on TV this week is *The Livid Mask*, a 1960 spectacular. . . ." But the column from which this was excerpted clearly stated that "the most watchable rerun" was not worth watching either.

Advertisements stress insignificant points for psychological appeal—the slightly faster rate of dissolving that one headache remedy has than another, the founding date of a company, or the fact that a beverage is imported rather than domestic. Such details often bear no relation to the overall quality of products so advertised.

Advertisers, labelers of products, and those preparing legal documents, warranties, etc. will sometimes place important material in fine print so that it is either not noticed, seemingly unimportant, or discouragingly tiring to read. Book clubs and record clubs offer in bold lettering several costly items for a couple of dollars, but, in fine print, bind the purchaser to a prescribed number of issues to be bought within the next year. One can hardly imagine a tobacco company placing the surgeon general's warning in bold type and relegating their claims of pleasure to smaller print. A whiskey label may read, "All of the Whiskies in This Blend Are Aged in Charcoal Kegs for Eight Years" and then in fine print reveal that only 25 percent or so of the content is whiskey while the rest is neutral spirits.

Often an argument will be presented with only items favorable to the argument being marshalled and negative or unfavorable points omitted. This neglecting of important aspects is a form of the fallacy of accent. It is illustrated by the isolationist arraignment of the United Nations which usually goes something like this.

> The United Nations was founded some thirty years ago to establish accord among nations, bring them together, and maintain world law and order. And what has happened? Nations have produced other nations as if by fission so that there are more nations than ever before. Then there was Vietnam. There has been war in the Middle East. There have been brushfires of violence in Africa. And now the United States seems to be trying to maintain peace unilaterally. I say let's pull out!

While the history of the United Nations is not entirely encouraging, such an argument neglects the importance of the United Nations as a continuing forum, what its subbodies have accomplished dealing with food, world health, and children, and other contributions of the organization to world peace and cooperation. It could be, of course, that a supporter of the United Nations might commit the fallacy

of accent by listing only favorable points about the organization and ignoring its weaknesses. In point of fact, however,
the latter rarely seems to happen.

Accent or inflection in oral expression slants the meanings of sentences. Repeat the statement "I hope you will
stay for lunch" four times, emphasizing in turn each of
the first three words and then the last word. "*I* hope you
will stay for lunch" may give away the fact that my wife
is not in so hospitable a mood. "I *hope* you will stay for
lunch" implies a sincere entreaty. "I hope *you* will stay for
lunch" may isolate others from the invitation. "I hope you
will stay for *lunch*" may seem to mean that a long visit
after lunch is not being urged.

Accent makes a great deal of difference in what readers
and listeners understand from statements. We will note
later on in connection with other types of fallacies that
*psychological* inference is very often not *logically* justifiable. Some philosophers, indeed, would urge that if we
adhere to careful principles of definition, psychological inference and logical inference would be defined as mutually
exclusive. In a practical sense it may be useful simply to
identify a particular inference as psychological and not
logical.

In the following instance there seems to be present a
psychological matter (rationalization) with an attempt to
justify it by an accent on a key word that is helpful to the
speaker's case. A minister gently took a parishioner to task
for gossiping. By way of admonishing the parishioner the
minister cited the Mosaic injunction, "Thou shalt not bear
false witness against thy neighbor." "Oh," rejoined the
man. "I'm not breaching that command. I haven't said
anything out of the way about my *neighbors!*"

Another church member sought to justify his accumu-
lation of wealth by pointing out that Jesus is quoted only

in part when it is said he urged, "Lay not up for yourselves treasures upon earth." This affluent layman notes correctly that the whole statement includes "where moth and rust doth corrupt and where thieves break through and steal." So, he goes on, "I'm investing in plastics that moths can't ruin and in government bonds that thieves would have a hard time getting at!"

### 5. Leading Questions, or Complex Questions

The leading or complex question is not to be confused with "begging the question," to be discussed in Chapter 5. An argument *begging* the question may be and usually is couched in affirmative language, with no question involved in it at all. The leading question is usually expressed as a question. But, it is one which implies something about an anticipated answer. "Why does a sports car with front wheel brakes make sense?" implies that such a braking arrangement does make sense. "Why is the world so unjust?" implies that the world is unjust. "What did you find so boring in class that you were yawning much of the time?" implies that the yawner was bored and not yawning for some other reason.

A complex question is one which may involve more than one question and imply more than one answer. Usually the complex question is stated to secure some answer favorable to the questioner and unfavorable to the respondent. Such is illustrated by the old saw, "Have you stopped beating your wife?" "Yes" implies that you did beat her in times past and "No" implies you are still administering beatings. "Have you been free of drug abuse for long?" puts one on a similar spot. Long ago Aristotle cautioned that several questions put as one "should be decomposed." Only a single question, he reasoned, admitted of a single answer.

Illustrations of the leading question are easy to come by.

A critic of his representative's position on tax reform asks, "Was it because he is controlled by special interests, has a vested interest in the legislation, or just plain stupid that Congressman Claggett voted 'No' on the tax reform bill?" A letter to an editor asks, "Why are you—or even the columnists who contribute to your paper—afraid to write about the problems concerning energy and the recession-inflation plight?"

"What makes a Synchromesh Camgear better?" not only implies that the Synchromesh Camgear is better—but it leaves us wondering, Better than what? Its earlier structure? Some other gear? Better than no gear at all?

A leading question is often a direct question prefaced by a bit of information or by an attempt at persuasion in the form of propositions. A plea for the reform of laws governing the dispensing of controlled drugs notes that in a given year enough people were arrested for involvement with marijuana in some way, often in a minor degree, to empty a large city. The question following this information is, "Don't you think it's time we stopped arresting people for using marijuana?"

A cigarette manufacturer who makes a cigarette which he claims has a low content of tar and nicotine raises the question in advertising as to what we are going to do about smoking. No doubt the desired answer to the question is not that we are going to stop smoking or even reduce our pack or more per day. The fairly obvious hope is that we will switch to the purportedly less harmful brand.

Similarly, but with a somewhat more constructive concern for our health, an organization concerned about Americans' tendency to excess body weight asks what we are *waiting* for. The question also involves a pun on *weight* and *wait,* an attention getting bit of equivocation.

## 6. ERRORS IN CONVERSION

Conversion means turning around. In its application in linguistic usage it is the process of turning a sentence around so that the subject becomes the predicate and the predicate becomes the subject. Two kinds of sentences can be converted easily. These are sentences involving "some are" and "none are." "Some assembly line workers are bored" becomes, upon conversion, "Some who are bored are assembly line workers." All that is necessary is to pivot the sentence at the verb.

The same is true of "none are" sentences. "No Fascists are Communists" becomes, when converted, "No Communists are Fascists." Since the statement indicates that Fascists and Communists are mutually exclusive it does not matter which is the subject and which is the predicate. In even stricter and more precise "logical" language, virtually essential to use when we get to syllogistic reasoning, these statements would read, "All Fascists are excluded from all Communists" and, in converted form, "All Communists are excluded from all Fascists." And, to return to the "some are" illustration concerning bored assembly line workers for a moment, the statements would read: "Some assembly line workers are included in bored persons" and "Some bored persons are included in assembly line workers."

Sentences involving "all are" require modification when they are converted. The modification is called "conversion by limitation." That is, the predicate must be limited by the word "some" when such a sentence is converted. Take, for example, the statement, "All housewives are concerned about inflation." To convert this sentence to read "All who are concerned about inflation are housewives" would

be to err in conversion. Clearly there are others than housewives who are concerned about inflation. The most that
can be said in converting "All housewives are concerned
about inflation" is that "Some who are concerned about
inflation are housewives." This should be quite clear, but
for emphasis let us use a somewhat different illustration.
Let us suppose that it is true that "All baseball players exercise daily." It certainly would not follow that "All who
exercise daily are baseball players." Tennis players, football players, swimmers and a host of other athletes may also
exercise daily.

"Some are not" propositions cannot be converted. "Some
truck drivers are not overpaid" cannot be converted to
"Some overpaid persons are not truck drivers." While both
statements may be true, neither can be derived from the
other. Suppose we had begun with the statement, "Some
overpaid persons are not truckdrivers." We could not convert this to read "Some truckdrivers are not overpaid persons." Let us use two circles to illustrate this situation.
Place one circle overlapping the other, one circle representing truckdrivers and the other overpaid persons.

The overlapping circles suggest three segments. Segment
one of the truckdrivers circle lies entirely outside the
circle of overpaid persons and this segment is declared
occupied by our proposition, "Some truckdrivers are not
overpaid." The "X" in this segment represents its being
occupied.

Segment two is that portion of the truckdrivers circle
overlapping the circle representing overpaid persons. But
this segment is not declared to be occupied. Neither is
segment three—that segment of the circle representing
overpaid persons which is not overlapped by the truckdrivers circle. Therefore when we say, "Some truckdrivers
are not overpaid" or "Some truckdrivers are excluded from

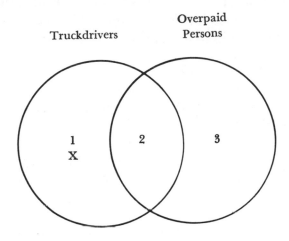

the overpaid," we cannot on the basis of that statement justify saying that there are any overpaid persons at all—truckdrivers or not.

Let us compare a perhaps even more obvious illustration with this one. Let us say, "Some men are not bachelors." We cannot convert this to "Some bachelors are not men," accepting for the purpose of this illustration the conventional definition of "bachelor" as being male.

Conversion is a helpful process at times, and so the error for which we must be watchful is erroneous conversion—the failure to limit the predicate when converting an "all are" proposition, or the attempt to convert a "some are not" proposition. Here are several further illustrations of errors in conversion.

The Mad Hatter, in one of Lewis Carroll's marvelous stories, challenged Alice on mishandling conversion, and in a slightly different form from that we have been considering. Upon being urged that she should say what she means, Alice protested that she means what she says—which, she says, is the same thing as saying what she means. This prompts the Mad Hatter to propose an analogy which belies his madness—that seeing what one eats is by no means the same as eating what one sees, and that liking what one gets is by no means the same as getting what one likes! We could reduce these propositions to inclusion thus: "All instances of meaning what one says are included in instances of saying what one means." Therefore "All instances of saying what one means are included in instances of meaning what one says." And so on. But that should be superfluous now.

If one infers from "All good politicians are extroverts" that "All extroverts are good politicians" he has clearly committed an error in failing to convert by limitation. Similarly one cannot conclude from "To be righteous is to really live" that "To really live is to be righteous," although it might be a noble aspiration to equate the two. "Good things come in small packages" does not assure one that a small package contains something good. Nor does the notion that great men write illegibly warrant the development of poor penmanship in the hope of attaining greatness.

## 7. ERRORS IN OBVERSION

Obversion is a procedure of direct inference in which the opposite of a given proposition is denied. This is accomplished by reversing the quality of a proposition (changing it from affirmative to negative or from negative to affirmative) without changing its quantity, that is, what is included or excluded.

The rule for proper obversion, then, is to change an affirmative connective verb to negative, or a negative connective verb to affirmative, and then to negate the predicate term. In obverting a proposition never negate the subject term.

Obversion is perhaps most often used for rhetorical or poetic effect and one wishing to think logically must be particularly sensitive to the possibility of misrepresentation of truth in rhetoric or poetry.

A veterans' organization speaker may declare with some justification, "All volunteers are patriotic." If he wishes he may put this another way by obverting it. He may say, "No volunteers are unpatriotic." But if in his fervor he says, "All volunteers are patriotic. Therefore, I tell you, all who do not volunteer are unpatriotic," he has committed a fallacy of obversion. Whether or not one agrees with such a statement of condemnation of all non-volunteers, "All who do not volunteer are unpatriotic" does not follow from the first statement, "All volunteers are patriotic" but his "therefore" declares that it does. Note that the error involves bringing into the second proposition a group—non-volunteers—who are not mentioned at all in the original proposition. What our veterans' speaker has done is to negate the subject and the predicate. This is not allowable in obversion.

The use of a set of three circles, one fairly large and two smaller ones, will illustrate the proper and improper forms of obversion. First the proper form. Let the large circle represent patriotic persons. And let one of the smaller circles represent volunteers and the other non-volunteers. Place the circle representing volunteers within the large circle. This depicts the proposition. "All volunteers are included in patriotic persons." The obverse of the proposition given is, "No volunteers are unpatriotic." That is, "No volunteers lie outside the circle of patriotic persons." This, then, is obvious.

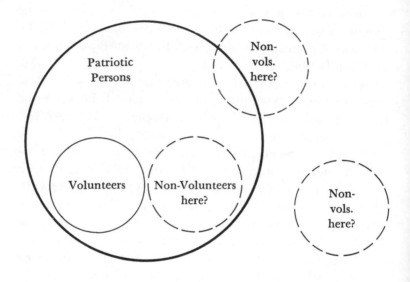

But what of non-volunteers? The small circle representing them may go inside the circle of patriotic persons, may lie partly within and partly without the circle of patriotic persons, or it may lie entirely outside the circle of patriotic persons. We simply do not know where to place this circle from what is given in the original statement.

The obverse of an "all are" proposition is a "no are non-" proposition—or "all are excluded from non-" proposition. "All voters are residents" becomes, when obverted, "No voters are non-residents," or "All voters are excluded from non-residents." If perchance one says, "No non-voters are residents," he has obverted improperly. Some non-voters may indeed be residents.

The obverse of a "some are" proposition is a "some are not non-" proposition. "Some voters are women" becomes, when obverted, "Some voters are not non-women," or "Some voters are excluded from all non-women."

The obverse of a "some are not" proposition is a "some are non-" proposition. Thus the obverse of "Some residents are not voters" is "Some residents are non-voters." Notice the change of the negative verb to affirmative and the negation of the predicate term by prefixing a simple "non-."

Proper obversion will involve clear negations—a negation of the verbal connective and a negation of the predicate by prefixing "non-" or "not-" rather than "un" or "in" where the latter imply a certain degree of uncertainty. Suppose you are seeking information about a candidate for a position and inquire, "Is Spadly trustworthy?" If you get the response, "Well, Spadly is not untrustworthy" you have less than an enthusiastic endorsement of the fellow. One should examine many other types of implied negation, too, like large/small, poor/rich, diligent/indolent and re-phrase any propositions where a middle ground must be ruled out. The length of a list of words to be given special consideration is prohibitively long as far as inclusion here is concerned. But the following is an illustrative sampling of terms that need to be clarified in regard to obversion:

| truthful | untruthful | not untruthful |
| moral | immoral | non-moral or amoral |
| human | inhuman | not inhuman |
| wise | unwise | not unwise |
| logical | illogical | not illogical |

Some who have already studied logic, an instructor in the area, for example, may question the inclusion of conversion and obversion in a section dealing with informal fallacies. It is correct that conversion and obversion are formal or logical processes. They are involved in direct, or immediate, inference. Given a single proposition how may it be re-expressed in some helpful ways without doing violence to the basic proposition? Therefore, conversion and obversion will be considered further in a chapter on direct inference. However, the tendency to err in converting and obverting propositions certainly has some psychological overtones and linguistic implications that link the practices with other topics in this chapter. This warrants their examination, therefore, in this context also.

## EXERCISES: CHAPTER 1

In this set of exercises and in the excercises for subsequent chapters selections are offered to illustrate fallacies discussed in the chapter which the exercises follow. Exercises may be presented in more than one chapter when they illustrate fallacies of more than one type.

Label the following according to the fallacy each most aptly illustrates.

1. An advertisement presents the words FIRST GRADE TIRE in inch-high lettering at the top of the advertisement and in somewhat smaller type gives prices, information about the structure of the tire, trade-in specifications, etc. Then in type much smaller even than regular news type states, "No standard has been set by industry or government for the designation First Grade Tire."

2. "All pacifists believe that broader economic and social planning is necessary. So I suppose that means

that all who believe in broader economic and social planning would be pacifists."

3. "How long are you going to persist in advocating policies set forth by an administration that has no vision of the nation's needs and has in its inner circle corrupt men?"

4. "Those whose consciences are clear suffer no pangs of remorse. Thus those whose consciences remind them of some wrong they have done must suffer remorse accordingly."

5. An old bit from vaudeville days has a character skipping back and forth across the stage, interrupting a stand-up comic's monologue. The comic asks why he is skipping. The reply: "The doctor told me to take some medicine three times daily and then skip a day."

6. Faculty member: "I have always been indefatigable in my efforts on behalf of aspiring, mature students. And whatever assiduous inquiry should reveal as potentially enhancing to attitudinal improvements in effectuating better intercommunication and continuing dialogue between students, faculty, and administration will have more than my tangential support."

7. "Senator Swilby has always boasted about being a liberal. Since he's liberal, let's hit him for $1,000 to help our kick-off for the United Fund."

8. "That's a lovely specimen of a cuckoopint!" "Cuckoopint? What's a cuckoopint?" "Oh, you know. It's a common European arum with lanceolate erect spathe and bright, usually purple, spadix."

9. Student to faculty member, discussing possible revisions in regulations: "What will you do to help us

get this policy about dormitory visitation changed?"

10. A bulletin board notice in a computer center office read: "The assistant manager has been assigned the task of redesigning the flow chart of responsibilities in this area so that in viewing the interrelation of units one will experience no difficulty whatever in getting confused."

11. An advertisement suggests that since one would not call a valuable antique piece of Hepplewhite "used furniture" one should not call their secondhand cars "used cars." "They are 'previously owned cars' and not 'used cars.' "

12. A beverage advertisement reads, "Where there's fun, there's plenty of Old Ziplein Ale." A shopper reacts, "Well, if we want to have fun at our party, we'd better stock up on Old Ziplein."

13. A presidential news secretary says, "No, our earlier statements were neither lies nor misrepresentations. It is simply that they are now inoperative."

14. During the 1968 presidential campaign a prominent figure in politics is reported to have said, "No sane person in this country likes the war in Vietnam, and neither does President Johnson."

15. Advertisement: "At the Floritz on the Strand the young are swinging to the music of the Earbusters. Their elders are swinging to Aulde Jack Whiskey. Why? It's a swinging kind of place."

16. The American Medical Association once circulated a brochure on medical, hospital, and surgical insurance. The booklet stated that full coverage in all three areas was available for less than $10.00 per month for a family. Upon investigation as to the source of such coverage an inquirer was told, "We only said 'full coverage.' We did not mean absolutely full coverage."

17. A college administrator opposed the establishment of a large community college system in a southeastern state. The editor of a newspaper invited him to prepare a column with byline presenting his position. The editor who strongly favored the development of the new colleges placed the article in ordinary type in the last column on the editorial page. In bolder than usual type the editor presented his own views in a double column spread on the left side of the editorial page.

18. Interviewer on television talk show: "There are several matters you have not mentioned in your comments. Why are you avoiding the subject of Russian fishing boats in waters near us?"

19. "You say your winters in this section are invigorating and healthful? Then I gather your other seasons must be debilitating and harmful to the health."

— 20. Freshman: "I've always been urged by my parents to do what is right. It is our right to cut as many non-test classes as we wish. So I'm cutting them all this week."

21. A circular offering for sale "ecology vitamins" lists among the contents of the capsules: "Amylytic enzyme, *Aspergillus niger*, proteolytic and cellulytic enzymes, cobalamin concentrate, rutin, hesperidin complex and L-Lysine."

22. "All students who made the dean's list have, by the record, CEEB score totals of 1200. You are not on the dean's list, so I suppose your total was less than 1200."

23. A political candidate impressed his hearers of the unworthiness of the incumbent opponent by proclaiming that his opponent was a blatant extrovert, that his sister was a thespian in wicked New York,

that he was a celibate before his marriage, and that
he practiced nepotism in his very office.

24. "Our founding fathers established a republican
form of government. It follows that the Republican
Party is the one we should support." "No. We live
in a democracy. Ours is a democratic government.
So we should be Democrats."

25. "All conservatives are wealthy and all Republicans
are conservatives so all wealthy people are Republicans."

26. "All who signed the petition are in favor of the investigation, obviously. So we must agree that any
who refuse to sign are against the investigation."

27. "Certainly the mayor will be rational in his discussion of this problem with us. After all, human
beings are rational animals. And the mayor is
generically a human being, so he will be rational."

28. "Could you tell me where to find the janitor?"
"Janitor? We don't have a janitor. But Mr. Smetner,
our custodian, is taking his break in the lounge."

29. "A man of wisdom is a man of years," observed an
English poet. "I would suppose, then, that wisdom
goes along with age—that older men are wise."

30. "You face not merely a dilemma but a polylemma.
And whether there is involved a *non sequitur* in
your analysis of the situation or not, a logical posi-
tivist is your best bet for indicating whether it is a
*non sequitur* or a metonymy or both."

COMMENTS ON EXERCISES FOR CHAPTER 1

1. Accent. Attention has been called, by the use of large
type placed at the heading of the advertisement, to
three words, "First Grade Tire," which would naturally appeal to an economy-minded customer for tires.

The smaller print indicates that "First Grade Tire" conveys no meaning whatever.

2.  An error in conversion. The fact—if it were a fact— that all pacifists believe in broader economic and social planning tells one nothing whatever about what a great many believers in economic and social planning think about the use or uses of violence.

3.  A leading or complex question. The question implies that the one questioned does advocate certain administrative policies. This has not been established, unless it was developed earlier in the dialogue. In that case, this would not serve as an illustration of a leading question.

4.  Erroneous obversion. What we are told about those with clear consciences does not reveal anything necessarily about those whose consciences are not clear.

5.  An instance of simple equivocation—a pun on the word "skip."

6.  Obscuration—with hardly any need for further comment.

7.  Equivocation. "Liberal" is used in two senses, one implying a political point of view and the other generosity with personal resources.

8.  Obscuration. In a conversation with the average person the definition of a "cuckoopint" would give no information whatever. The average person would very likely think that a bird was involved. A botanist, however, would not necessarily find the definition obscure. Words like "arum," "spathe," and "spadix" would be readily known to him and describe quite aptly a kind of plant.

9.  A leading question, implying that the faculty member is ready to lend a helping hand in getting policies changed.

10. An amphiboly. The sequence of words implies that the flow chart will assist one in getting confused, which is surely not the intent of the announcement.

11. The expression "previously owned" for "used" is euphemistic. It sounds somewhat better, but one should not be misled into thinking a "previously owned" car has not been used and possibly used rather extensively.

12. A shopper reasoning thus is not reasoning well. He is committing the error of false conversion. "All places where there's fun are included in places where there's plenty of Old Ziplein Ale" (even if such an absurd claim were made) cannot be converted to "All places where there's plenty of Old Ziplein Ale there's fun."

13. A rather well-known euphemistic expression.

14. An amphibolous statement which is easily construed as implying that President Johnson was to be excluded from the sane.

15. Equivocation—with two meanings of "swinging" being employed.

16. A rather unusual form of equivocation. Should one use a comparative form of words like "full," "unique," etc.?

17. A clear case of the fallacy of accent. The favorable positioning and the larger type were apparently designed to attract attention and to utilize an editorial advantage, a common practice, however regrettable.

18. A complex question—to the extent that there may be a shade of difference between the leading question and the complex question. In the talk show many matters may have consumed the actual time of the questioner so that the person being interviewed would have had to change the subject to mention the situation he has now been charged with avoiding!

19. An error in obversion. Nothing was said in the initial

statement about the spring, the summer, or the fall seasons.

20. Equivocation, since "right" is clearly used in two different senses: a. what is good, proper, correct, or morally acceptable; and b. a privilege.

21. Obscuration, for to those having neither training in pharmacology nor devotion to medical columns in journals the terminology is highsounding and perhaps euphemistic, but by our definition rather obscure.

22. Erroneous obversion. The initial statement says nothing about those not on the dean's list.

23. The speaker, very likely by the use of inflection, has given to one rather rarely used word, thespian, the apparent meaning of a word that for many has undesirable connotations, lesbian. He has also left the impression that extroversion, celibacy, and nepotism are undesirable when such qualities may be quite acceptable in particular situations.

24. Equivocation. Clearly the speakers have not decided how they will define the words "republican" and "democratic," each of which can be used in several ways.

25. An error in conversion. When the predicate of an affirmative proposition beginning with "all" is shifted to the position of subject, the quantifying word "some" must replace the "all."

26. False or erroneous obversion.

27. Equivocation, with rational having two meanings.

28. "Custodian" is an increasingly used euphemism for "janitor."

29. An error in conversion. In stricter logical phrasing this is clear: "All wise men are included in older men" and therefore "All older men are included in wise men." Hardly, alas.

30. A concocted illustration of obscuration.

# Chapter 2

# Misdirected Thinking

Sometimes we ourselves digress from strictly logical thinking when we allow distracting ideas to color subtly our psychological processes. And, of course, we have to watch lest others use verbal sleight of hand to divert thinking from issues at hand. Those tactics to be discussed in this chapter are perhaps the most frequently encountered diversionary devices although they are by no means all. Consider such arguments as the following. Do they make sense?

"Your vote to revoke the sales tax on necessities will bankrupt the state, halt our roadbuilding, destroy our educational system, and bring on ruin," argues a member of a budget commission.

In debating an issue concerning the committee structure of a newly established organization one man said to another, "Your arguments remind me of what my dad said about hoopskirts. They swished round and round and never touched on anything worthwhile!"

"Yes, this generation of young people reads more poorly than those in their comparable social ranks of earlier decades. And I know television is to blame. No other cause has been discovered and no one has proved television blameless."

"How can you trust him for a minute about anything? He was once employed by the CIA as an infiltrator of and informer on the Ku Klux Klan. And then he turned right around and squealed on the CIA before a senate committee.

We will return to these arguments after examining the various fallacies of diversion in some detail.

## 1. Extension

Extension is the running of an argument or line of reasoning into the ground, to use the popular figure of speech for such a procedure. When one introduces irrelevant extremes into a discussion he is committing the fallacy of extension.

A father, discussing his son's prospective purchase of a foreign car, cautions, "Remember the foreign cars we have had? We had some small but very irritating, time-consuming trouble with every last one of them. Remember how hard ordinary parts were to locate at times?" The son, who has his mind firmly set on a Fortinita says, "Aw, dad, you think the Fortinita will fall completely apart like the deacon's wonderful one horse shay!" The son has extended the father's caution from his mention of small, irritating details to complete simultaneous collapse of all parts.

A political science student says, "With our large population and closed frontiers, economic planning is going to be increasingly necessary." A business major objects, "So you think we might as well go completely Communist, eh?" A case of extension again.

In a discussion of the questions related to drug abuse someone says, "Sentencing a young man for 'attempted possession of illegal drugs' means that soon we will be jailing people for fantasizing or even dreaming about smoking grass." There may be serious moral and legal questions concerning the case that precipitated the discussion, but it does not help the analysis to extend one's imagination so far about future results of court actions.

An advocate of socialism raises an issue thus: "If free enterprise capitalism is so blasted wonderful, why is it that it leads with appalling regularity to recession, depression, 'stagflation'—whatever you want to call it? Capitalism will not only continue to cause such economic troubles but some day will collapse ruinously under the weight of its own inherent faults." The argument has been foreshortened in its omissions and extended as regards its conclusion.

A comparable instance of committing the fallacy of extension comes from an ardent anti-socialist who was defending free enterprise capitalism to the point where he was severely critical of detente with communist nations. "Detente with Russia especially," he argued, "means capitalism is through, Christianity is through, America is through, and civilization is through."*

President Ford in an appearance at Notre Dame University directed some criticism at those who opposed his request for further military assistance to South Vietnam while that country was retreating from onslaughts of the enemy. Whatever the merits of his case, he rather overdrew the picture of some of his critics when he said, "Some counsel us to withdraw from one world and go it alone."

---

*"Detente," traditionally meaning a relaxation of tensions between nations, in 1976 became tarnished with the meaning of disadvantageous stalemate. The campaigning incumbent president tried to eliminate the word from political debate.

Such extreme isolationists are quite rare and without much of a public forum. So he must have been directing his remarks at political figures who are heard virtually throughout the land none of whom have urged quite such a stringent withdrawal.

Two illustrations of more individual than national or international moment conclude the list of illustrations of extension. A father was trying to explain to his son why mandatory wearing of helmets for motorcycle riders is good. "Without a helmet you have no protection for the most vulnerable part of your body," he said. "Even the consequences of a small misjudgment could be fatal without a helmet." The son retorts, "Why don't they make us wear a helmet every time we go outside the house? I wonder when they will make bike riders wear medieval coats of armor?"

A woman was in conference with her pastor about her husband who was spreading his affections about somewhat—to use a euphemism. The minister drew upon the New Testament injunction that one should forgive not once, nor even seven times, but seventy times seventy. "What?" she exclaimed, "I know of three or four other times he's stepped out on me and there may be still some others. Do you mean I still have to put up with 480-odd affairs?"

## 2. Misuse of Humor

There are many, many times when a touch of humor has a place in discourse, even in debate and argument. But it should be appropriate to the setting or theme under discussion and used mainly to relieve tension or tedium. Humor is improperly used when it diverts attention from the issues, or when it distorts unfairly some point in the deliberations.

In analyzing equivocation in Chapter 1 the interruption of a line of reasoning by a pun upon the word "conceive" was reported. "I know you cannot conceive. You're a man." The sally was entirely irrelevant and terminated further serious discussion.

A similar misuse of humor, based upon equivocation, is the response someone made to the suggestion, "Now let's just look at the president's overall record, not just the blunders even he admits he has made." The rejoinder was, "There is no need to. He wanted to be president in the worst way—and he sure is!" This rejoinder seems to have been adapted, by the way, from that same president's defeated opponent who said on one occasion, "I wanted to run for president in the worst way—and I did." The use of humor was somewhat more appropriate in the original context.

One needs to be careful about the use of humor not only as an unfair diversionary tactic but also because sometimes one may intend to use it for some point and have it lead to disaster. One such instance was that in which a speaker not only failed to score a point with his audience but actually lost favor with many of his hearers. A news commentator had addressed a university audience on the controversial Vietnam issue and was engaged in a question and answer period. A faculty member who was known by the audience, but not by the speaker, to have had some two decades of military service in southeast Asia asked a sincere question, "Do you have information on this particular point that the secretary of state and the secretary of defense may not have?" "No," the speaker replied. "I'm just smarter than they are." The audience's laughter was moderate and its groans quite audible and the speaker's attempt to further defend his judgment was largely unsuccessful.

Hecklers are a hazard to more than stand-up comics. They can spoil the line of thought of a teacher, a politician, or anyone who delivers them an opening. A professor had a class that was singularly lacking in historical curiosity. Hoping to impress upon his students the importance of historical knowledge he asked one day, "Suppose we define history in a very broad sense as a record of everything that has ever happened, significant or not. Suppose, further, you awake some morning with complete amnesia. You cannot remember a single thing that you have ever experienced or read about. What would you do?" The prompt, memorable reply was hardly the one hoped for. The response of a student was, "I'd turn over and go back to sleep."

However, humor certainly has a place in human communication. It is sometimes a psychological relief when it is used following a failure of humor designed for a good cause. Such is a case involving Russia's campaign against cigarette smoking. Someone in the Soviet Union has revealed a sense of humor in their anti-smoking posters. One has the serpent offering Eve a pack of cigarettes instead of the legendary apple. Another shows God wearing a gas mask for protection against clouds of smoke rising from the earth, with God opining, "There's only one way out, another flood." A member of the staff of *Krokodil* was asked if the posters were effective. He answered, "Well, no. Not much. You see, it's so hard to see them for the smoke!"

### 3. Appeal to Ignorance, or Argumentum ad Ignorantiam

The appeal to ignorance, or the *argumentum ad ignorantiam*, is a rather peculiar line of so-called reasoning to adopt. One would think that a rational person, or one who styled himself as rational, would not appeal to the absence of any knowledge whatever to adduce proof of something. But somehow our minds tend to play tricks on us and permit us to set forth conjecture as fact—since no other conjecture or evidence refutes it—defend faith in the most difficult to accept forms, and assess guilt not only where proof beyond a shadow of doubt is lacking but because the absence of proof seems somehow to substantiate our claim.

It is clearly an appeal to ignorance to claim that extremes of weather over a two-year period resulted from a space laboratory and other satellites circling our globe. "There is no evidence to the contrary, so the various man-made satellites must be drastically affecting our weather," a number of persons have argued.

A speaker who was more articulate than logical supported the notion of the immortality of the soul thus: "The human soul is immortal for no one has produced clear evidence that the spirit which is characteristic of man does not survive after the death of the body."

Psychologists square away on matters like PSI factors—extrasensory perception, clairvoyance, psychokinesis, and the like—arguing against each other on the basis of ignorance. Those favoring PSI factors argue, "You have no evidence supporting other causative factors than those we propose, so our assertions are valid." Opponents of that position argue, "Telepathy, clairvoyance and psychokinesis are sheer nonsense since their validity has not been clearly demonstrated."

Similarly some of those evaluating senatorial investigations in the Watergate affair argued on the one side that the president was innocent of charges of wrongdoing since proof had not been established as to his guilt and some argued on the other that the president was guilty of charges of wrongdoing since he had taken no adequate steps to prove his innocence.

In a democracy it is of utmost importance to hold to the principle that one alleged to have committed a crime is innocent until proved guilty. In a strict sense, however, judges and juries are following precise logical principles when they announce a verdict of "not guilty" rather than a verdict of "innocent."

As has been noted, two or more fallacies are sometimes closely linked. The *post hoc* fallacy ("After this therefore because of this" as discussed in Chapter 3) is linked with questionable reasoning about satellites and weather, for the run of strange weather certainly followed in time sequence the launching of the satellites. The fact that meteorological records may show earlier periods of similar weather trends is ignored, of course, in such thinking. Arguments about the president's innocence or guilt, as above, will have an *ad hominem* flavor, argument from the character of the man, discussed in section 5 of this chapter. Here are a few more illustrations.

Despite the elaborate preparations for placing men on the moon and the considerable publicity given the preparations there were still skeptics who said in one phrasing or another: "You can't prove to me they landed. I wasn't along. There are too many ways to doctor a film to make it look like they made a landing."

Another that has to do with science pertains to the effect the diffusion of freon into the atmosphere might have upon ozone. "Freon destroy the ozone in our atmosphere? No one has yet calculated accurately how much freon is released from spray can usage, refrigeration production, and that sort of thing—and matched it against the ozone surrounding us. So what? Me worry?"

A naturalist recently observed, one supposes and hopes

facetiously, "Folk wisdom has told us for centuries that a bag of garlic cloves will protect one from werewolves. And so far as I can discover no one has adduced a shred of evidence to the contrary."

And what community is spared allegations that someone is in a position to make money from some public project with the allegations based upon the absence of some data that might be pertinent. Thus a news-radio station owner was led to respond to such criticisms in this manner: "It has been said that some of those favoring the construction of a nearby airport will make money out of its construction. I would like to see any of you produce one bit of documented evidence that anyone other than John Q. Public will benefit." And so he answered critics in kind.

## 4. APPEAL TO FORCE, OR ARGUMENTUM AD BACULUM

*Argumentum ad Baculum* is a very apt expression for appeal to force for the Latin term *baculum* means rod. And any time a rod, physically or figuratively, is used instead of cogent reasoning and explanation, the fallacy of appeal to force is involved.

Some instances of the appeal to force are gross departures from logic. "Your money or your life" involves a decision to be made, but hardly logic as such. And, indeed, the appeal to force may be somewhat more psychological than logical in any situation in which it is used. But logicians tend to analyze the fallacy anyway.

The rod, or *baculum,* may derive from parental authoritarianism in which something a little reasonable may be involved. "If your grades don't improve, you won't get the use of the car all next quarter" is, of course, a threat. And yet the threat may imply, not entirely unreasonably, that social affairs have developed to such an extent that they overshadow study habits.

The rod may be the application of economic pressure,

as when a sales manager says to his sales force, "You either meet your quota this month—regardless of financial conditions hereabouts, the quality of our advertising programs or anything else—or you'll be looking for another job. Produce or else."

The rod may be political or military force or a combination of them, as when Stalin, when head of the USSR, questioned including the Pope in discussions of international affairs. He asked, "How many military divisions does the Pope have?" If this was not an implied threat to the Pope to stay in his place, it was an implication that only those who could appeal to force should join in the making of treaties.

A more recent illustration of an approximation to the appeal to force was the response of former Secretary of State Kissinger to a question as to what measures he thought should be taken to assure continuing oil supplies from oil producing countries to the more highly industrialized nations. He said, in effect, that in the event oil availability is reduced so as to threaten strangulation of industry, armed intervention might not be omitted from consideration. The grim realities of the mood of men and nations may have justified some such inverted or negatively stated observation. But the psychological impact of the observation was such as to dramatize for illustrative purposes the implied appeal to force.

One who wishes to stand committed to the canons of logic is sometimes placed in a strained situation contending with the maxim credited to Fontaine's *Fables:* "The reasoning of the strongest is always the best."

### 5. Appeal Against the Man, or Argumentum ad Hominem

Other names for this type of fallacy include *Tu Quoque* ("You too!") and *Genetic Fallacy*. Nitpickers or pettifoggers—a discussion of which follows shortly—may quibble over whether or not the three expressions just given for a particular type of fallacy should be grouped together. Their specific occurrences are so numerous and so shaded into various meanings as to provide material for a long dissertation on them severally or together. The grouping, then, is for the sake of brevity and to assure that students are cued in on something wrong when someone: (1) Argues that someone is the kind of man who would (or would not) say so and so or do so and so. (2) Says, "You do or say so and so, so why shouldn't I?" (3) Argues from the nature of the origin or association of data, deed or discourse the merit or lack of merit of such data, deed or discourse.

Argument against, or in terms of the nature of, the man is illustrated in the university trustee's remark, "We can expect Assistant Professor Le Sage to vote for the liberalized plan for tenure and promotion. After all, he's still on the way up in the teaching profession." Or the conservative movie fan who says, "No more Jane Fonda pictures for me after her anti-war speeches and criticism of prisoners of war! No one who says such things could possibly be a competent actress." Or the liberal who says, "No, I don't care for Sammy Davis' performances any more since he switched his politics." Or one placing a bet against Mohammed Ali in a heavyweight match saying, "He was a draft evader, is cocky, spouts corny rhymes, runs down his opponents, and even changed his religion for publicity purposes. He can't last as a fighter and this bout will prove it."

*Tu quoque,* or "You too," is usually a defense mechanism, as when a patient leaving his doctor's office protested, "But, doc, you smoke! Why can't I?" It might be well if the doctor set a good example, but at least he was correct in pointing out, "Look, you are paying me to help you take care of your health, not mine." Another illustration: Former President Nixon and his supporters defended various instances of taping and bugging conversations on the ground that earlier administrations followed the practice; they soft pedaled Nixon's tax problems while playing up deep freezers and vicuna coats in an earlier administration; and they cited earlier presidents' political use of the CIA and FBI to justify Nixon's apparent tampering with those organizations.

For a further sampling of the varied types of the *ad hominem* argument, examine the following illustrations.

Students in a college community were exercised at the attempts of some law enforcement officials to deal with what seemed to be a drug problem especially on the campus. Students themselves admitted, by the way, that various kinds of drugs were readily available. But one of their number wrote a letter to the editor of a local paper which went like this: "It is easy to see why the sheriff is now making a push against drug pushers, especially among students. He is up for re-election and students are particularly easy targets. They are involved in a college situation, far from home and their parents pose no threat on the local political scene. The students, too, for the most part cannot qualify to vote locally."

Occasionally the *ad hominem* argument is directed inward. "Who are we to complain about Russia's 'thought control' over writers and artists? Look at the repressive Greek and Spanish regimes we support! They surely do exercise thought control over *their* writers and artists!"

Sometimes one reasons in reverse order from something about a man's practice to conjectures as to the cause. A student said, for example, "Professor Le Sage certainly does work us hard and tends to be very dogmatic. That kind of fellow must either have had a repressed childhood or be henpecked at home!"

Turning to history, an occasional figure might well be eliminated from study. For example, the framer of a syllabus for a sociology course said, "Rousseau was an exhibitionist, exposing his posterior to ladies being his special delight. He is believed to have had an illegitimate child which he placed in a foundling home. Certainly no attention should be paid to his educational and social theories."

A critic of the Washington scene, albeit a member of congress, stated in an interview, "All of the officials in Washington cannot tell you how many committees, bureaus and offices there are in the federal government. No wonder they cannot tell us how to balance the budget." (First, note, we have a vague proposition—to be analyzed in Chapter 9. Does he mean "All of the officials in Washington are excluded from those who can tell how many committees, etc., there are?" Or does he mean, "Some of the officials in Washington" cannot impart immediately this information?) But the main point here is that because an official does not know one specific bit of statistical data he cannot shed light on a general problem to which the bit of information relates. And on a currently warmly debated issue we hear the question frequently raised, "How can you presume to debate the matter of abortion ethics and laws? You aren't a woman."

Sometimes the *argumentum ad hominem* may be urged as a basis for reaching a negative conclusion, as disproving something. Such was the case when a lawyer pled with a jury, "Look at the mother before you, her gentle, lovely face seamed with lines of care. Look at her fine son, a successful businessman, and her daughter with a child of her own. Think back to the happy family of their childhood, laughing around a Christmas tree, or excitedly enjoying a birthday party. How could anyone even think of this woman, epitome of motherhood and upright womanhood, committing even the smallest crime?"

The genetic fallacy, as customarily encountered, is very close kin to appeal to authority or association with honored men or sources, discussed in Chapter 4. When Jesus was condemned by the Pharisees for healing on the Sabbath he replied that anyone of them would have hauled an ox from the ditch to save it even on the Sabbath. He was using the "you too" approach. And then we follow this up, committing the genetic fallacy, when we appeal to this story to justify a variety of kinds of work we want to do on the Sabbath.

### 6. PETTIFOGGING, OR NIT-PICKING

The terms pettifogging and nit-picking are unpleasant terms given to unpleasant informal fallacies. They label one of the more annoying devices for diverting attention from main lines of reasoning, for often pettifogging is a prickly attack upon the one who is advancing an argument and tends to be more of a personal irritant than a diversion that one might innocently engage in. For example, two men were discussing the developments which led to the establishment of the People's Republic of China. One of them, whose interpretation of history was being challenged by the other, suddenly said, "There, now. You see. You don't even know how to pronounce Chiang Kai-shek's name correctly! I studied Chinese for a year and here's how his name is pronounced." He followed up his purportedly accurate pronounciation, which differed somewhat from the commonly anglicized pronunciation, saying,

"No use my talking with someone who can't pronounce a proper name in Chinese correctly!"

Perhaps it is the psychological factor that has led logicians in general to ignore the fallacy and omit it from their texts. But it is included here as a caution that about the only way to counter pettifogging is with patience and the hope that an opponent will yield, when pettifogging is politely noted, and move back to important issues.

Or perhaps pettifogging as such has received little treatment because the one who resorts to pettifogging has mastered the fallacies in reasoning such as those in Part 1 of this text into the questionable art of perverse argumentation. He will watch for double meanings to seize upon, he will offer a complex question, he will convert or obvert falsely, he will attempt humor, and he will set forth fallacies we have not yet discussed in order to divert attention or score over a participant in a discussion.

He will also quibble over precise definition, by invoking the dictionary or challenging the dictionary; over grammatical structure, by citing a textbook or correcting a textbook; over spelling, by invoking McGuffey or Webster or denying that either is an authority; or over historical detail, by pitting historiographer against historiographer. Indeed, there is no picayunish detail that escapes the accomplished pettifogger.

Before we proceed with the exercises for this chapter let us return to the illustrations of fallacies which introduced the chapter. The speaker concerned with the sales tax has quickly run an argument into the ground—has engaged in extension.

The analogy suggested about a debate being like a hoopskirt is a misuse of humor. The arguments supporting the notion that television is to be credited with poor read-

ing involve the appeal to ignorance. And the criticism of
the erstwhile CIA employee is an *ad hominem* argument.

Exercises: Chapter 2

Label the following according to the fallacy each most
aptly illustrates.
1.  A pacifist was pressing a retired army major on prin-
    ciples of Christian ethics and finally asked him, "What
    do you make of Jesus' command to love our enemies?"
    "Oh, I love my enemies," replied the major. "I love to
    kill them."
2.  Motorist to patrolman: "I worked right hard in the
    last campaign for Mayor Frizzo, and the majority on
    the city council had my support too, and they know it.
    May I suggest you just tear up that little old ticket?"
3.  "You certainly wouldn't consider Doakley as super-
    visor. He has had a couple of sessions with a shrink."
4.  "The alarmists have not been able to prove that radio-
    active fallout is sufficient to endanger human life.
    Therefore the test ban treaty is nonsense."
5.  "I'm not about to boycott beef. First thing you know
    everybody will be doing it and this would wreck our
    whole economy."
6.  Abraham Lincoln once asked a heckler: "Suppose I
    call a horse's tail a leg. How many legs would he then
    have?" "Five," came the answer. "No he wouldn't,"
    Lincoln said. "No matter what we call a horse's tail,
    it's still a tail."
7.  "Those patterned signals from outer space! Since we
    have not identified any other source for them, they
    must come from intelligent life."
8.  "As an editor you should be more accurate in your
    writing. In a recent editorial you used the phrase

'guild the lily.' You should know Shakespeare's expression was 'gild refined gold and paint the lily'!"

9. A minister was defending his position as an ardent
militarist and told the following story. "Sam Jones,
old time Georgia evangelist, was asked by a village
cynic if he believed everything that was in the Bible.
'Yes,' said the Reverend Jones, 'from cover to cover.'
'And you do what it says?' 'Yes. I try.' 'You mean if
I hit you on one cheek you'd turn the other?' 'Yes, I
would.' Whereupon the man landed a sound blow on
Brother Jones' cheek. Mr. Jones smiled, rubbed his
cheek, and turned the other one. The man hit it a
hard blow, too. Thereupon the Reverend Jones said,
'And that's as far as the Bible goes.' And he gave
the man a licking!"

10. Wife: "Do you really think you should have a fourth
highball?" Husband: "Listen! You want I should be
a teetotaler?"

11. "No, I cannot vote for him for governor. His father
amassed a fortune from whiskey."

12. For several years a rather large industrial organization
quietly circulated reports that if a union were voted
in at one of their plants the recreational facilities—
lake, tennis courts, golf course, etc.—available free to
workers and their families, would be closed.

13. "No slight scandal has ever been pinned on Congressman Stratelace. I'm sure he's never had any kickbacks
or been guilty of any indiscretions of any sort."

14. Teacher: "In view of your low grades to date, I think
you should do some serious studying before the examination."
Student: "If you expect me to do nothing but study
until exam time, you are expecting much too much."

15. "You say Professor Le Sage is an intellectual? Huh!

In his syllabus he has impughn for impug. He either can't spell or can't proofread. So, he's no intellectual."

16. "He's a retired colonel who served in the engineering corps for many years in southeast Asia. I know right now, without hearing his speech, how he stands on our military action in Vietnam. He's for it."

17. The president of a college in rather straitened financial circumstances passed the following note to the chairman of the committee on readmissions: "I'm quite aware that Joe Mabe is considerably below the standards we have set for readmission. But his father is one of our wealthier trustees who has hinted at a $250,000 donation to our new science building. It would be well if you could make an exception in Joe's case."

18. Lawyer: "Aha! You must free the defendant. The charges say the murder weapon was a 'Smith and Western' pistol. There is no such thing. 'Smith and Wesson,' yes. But, 'Smith and Western,' no."

19. "I am in favor of increasing our exports for it will improve our balance-of-payments situation." "I'm not! It will mean the rich in our country will become fabulously richer, that we of the middle class will be financial cripples, and the poor will starve."

20. Spelvin was convicted of cheating, the student council recalling that he had been up before them on other occasions, once on charges of speeding, and again, prior to changes in regulations pertaining to alcohol, for having a six pack of beer in his room.

21. Car owner to insurance adjuster: "Yes, I know you have to look carefully to even see the scratch on the bumper. But it was put there in the accident and my insurance covers it. I don't care if it does cost an additional ninety bucks. And if you don't include it

in the repairs, well, just try to sell any insurance in my neighborhood!"

22. A candidate for national office on the democratic ticket finally became quite edgy because of what he believed to be unfair tactics on the part of his opponents. So he responded quietly to a heckler as he left a meeting, using an oft spoken epithet. Questioned later an aide responded, "Well, you would not expect him to say, 'Kiss my elephant', would you?"

23. A rental agency quietly got the word to a restaurant operator that if he did not effectively discourage Blacks from patronizing his business, his lease would not be renewed.

24. "You say I'm appealing to ignorance in saying that the news media is controlled by a radical group, and backed by leftists who are also moneyed Jews! Let me see you prove it's not!"

25. "It's ridiculous to limit beer sales to those over eighteen. Don't you know that even Snow White served drinks to miners?"

### COMMENTS ON EXERCISES FOR CHAPTER 2

1. In a sense this illustrates, or is intended to illustrate, misuse of humor. In the context in which the dialogue was heard the remark would be termed these days as a cruel joke type of humor.

2. The citizen speaking to the patrolman is bringing the force of his influence to bear to avoid receiving a ticket. This illustrates appeal to force.

3. Appeal against, or in terms of one aspect of the nature of, the man. One who has submitted to psychological therapy could be more fitted for office by virtue of such treatment than his opponent might be.

4. The appeal to ignorance.

5. An extension of an argument beyond reasonable bounds.
6. Abraham Lincoln, for all of his many fine qualities, was gifted at the use of, and often abuse of, logic. In this case, possibly apocryphal, he was abusing the use of humor.
7. Appeal to ignorance.
8. Nit-picking or pettifogging. An editor's use of a widely misquoted and misspelled item from Shakespeare should not detract unduly from a line of argument he might be presenting.
9. For the pacifistically inclined this would be a blatant misuse of humor. For those as militaristic as the minister likely was, this would be a very clever proper use of humor.
10. The tippling husband has engaged in extension. His wife has requested only moderation, not abstinence.
11. *Argumentum ad hominem.*
12. *Argumentum ad baculum.*
13. *Argumentum ad hominem.* One should not, of course, infer that when an appeal has been made to ignorance that Congressman Stratelace is guilty of any indiscretions. What may or may not be inferred from a single proposition is the subject of a chapter to follow later in this work.
14. The student is right, we might well assume, that he should not be expected to do nothing but study for the rest of the term—but he is abusing the situation by extending considerably the teacher's suggestion.
15. Nit-picking.
16. The tendency to stereotype, as in this case, is a form of the *argumentum ad hominem.*
17. A subtle appeal to force.
18. Nit-picking. But sometimes a lawyer succeeds in

establishing his position by such procedures that breach the canons of logic while taking advantage of the vagaries of law.

19. Extension.
20. *Ad hominem.*
21. This is a nonfictional instance of a kind of nitpicking that very likely promotes inflation in automobile insurance rates.
22. This is an instance of using humor in an attempt to soften the impact of slightly abusive language. Whether it is a misuse or not may be debated. It could also be debated as to whether or not in the long run it would be better if aides let the fragility of their sensitive candidates stand to reflect to their credit.
23. A blatant appeal to force.
24. The speaker here persists in appealing to ignorance.
25. A questionable use of humor based upon a simple ambiguity, a play upon the similarity of sounds of the words "minors" and "miners."

# Chapter 3

# Omission of Relevant Data

In addition to problems arising from inaccurate use of language and from digressions from straight lines of thinking, we often encounter errors that arise from omitting data that is pertinent to a situation.

"We've got to get rid of this infernal welfare program," says a merchant. "Only this morning I went down to Blight Street looking for some temporary help in shipping and receiving, and I was turned down three times by loafers. Welfare's destroying willingness to work. It's ruining the country, I tell you."

Tourists report that shopkeepers, hotel managers, and people in general in many countries think, "America is a wealthy country and therefore this visitor, since he's from America, must be rolling in money."

"Several times in recent history wars erupted during Democratic administrations and peace was established during Republican administrations. The conclusion is obvious. If you want peace, vote Republican."

These quotations represent only three of at least nine types of thinking from which there may have been omitted some significant data. We will take another look at them at the conclusion of this chapter.

Our day by day lives would be rather sorely cluttered if we attempted to apply the scientific method, on which we so pride ourselves, rigorously to every decision we had to make, for the scientific method goes something like this. One must first recognize a problem, and this is the only really easy step. Then one must proceed along these lines: (1) Assemble any data that would appear even offhand to be relevant to the problem. (2) Organize the data into a pattern or into patterns that might shed some light on the problem. (3) State a hypothesis or several hypotheses that might be examined, and in certain kinds of situations tested, to aid in arriving at a solution to whatever the problem is. This can often be a long, involved process.

Fortunately even in our technological age we are not required to determine every decision we make by such a tedious procedure. One phase of it, however, should always be on the threshold of one's awareness: the need for data. The present chapter will deal with several types of error involving the omission of or the slighting of data.

## 1. ACCIDENT, OR THE FALLACY OF THE GENERAL RULE

The fallacy of accident consists in moving from a generally accepted rule or principle to a special case—a case that lacks the features of cases to which the rule generally applies, or a case which is quite different from the general run of cases. To reason that since democracy is the best form of government yet devised by man therefore it should be the government of Watsuvia, which is just developing a national awareness and organization, would be to commit the fallacy of accident. It might be that democracy requires some intermediate or evolutionary steps before it becomes a national practice. To say that aspirin is useful for the relief of headaches in general and therefore it should be used for a specific headache is also to commit the fallacy of accident. One would do well to know something about the cause of his headache and whether or not aspirin may aggravate the background condition.

The fallacy of accident, like many other fallacies in logic, is the basis for some little word games or jokes. An example, dating apparently from antiquity, continues to be perpetuated in logic books: "What you bought at the grocery store today you will eat tomorrow. You bought a dozen raw eggs today. Therefore, you will eat a dozen raw eggs tomorrow."

This bit of trivia, however, is analogous to the way we sometimes reason about important issues involved in legislation. "The land use legislation currently before the senate proposes limitations and controls on the way land may be developed for use. Therefore, in a short time every homeowner and farmer will find restrictions on rights to use his land as he wants to, rights which have come down from the Anglo-Saxons." This argument ignores the fact that such legislation may not be retroactive to apply to established, specific, small areas of ownership but only to developments that affect wide areas of land or the resources like streams that lie even beyond those areas. This argument also commits the fallacy of extension.

In the recurring debate over gun control laws one frequently reads or hears: "Our constitution declared the right of the citizenry to keep and bear arms. I have every right to a .38 caliber pistol! So, as a matter of fact, do you and Pete Ramus and Joseph Doakes and everyone else." It should be clear, but apparently it is not, that in consideration of any regulation or registration of weapons one should examine what our founding fathers had in mind in providing for a militia, what social factors determine the use to which individuals may put weapons and several other factors. To take the general notion that the constitution reserved to the citizenry the right to have and bear arms and apply that to various specific instances is to commit the fallacy of accident.

## 2. CONVERSE ACCIDENT, OR HASTY GENERALIZATION

Just as in the fallacy of accident one moves from the general to the specific in an inappropriate way, so in the fallacy of converse accident or hasty generalization one moves from specific instances, usually too few, to state a general rule. A common expression for the fallacy is "jumping to a conclusion."

Critics of minority groups, organizations seeking social change, and political figures furnish convenient illustrations of this fallacy. Members of minority groups, too, even though they often espouse good causes, frequently generalize too hastily about those they wish to challenge. Almost no person or group is exempt from victimization by the fallacy.

"Women are poor drivers," "Professors are absent-minded," "Blacks have an inborn sense of rhythm," "Poets lack common sense," and "Politicians are dishonest" are notions very likely derived from hasty generalizations. When a labor union went on strike during wartime the charge was widely circulated, "All union members are unpatriotic!" Again, converse accident.

Variations on this theme are numerous. In the moral realm we reason, "Decades of readers have honored 'The Other Wise Man' in Van Dyke's story, and he lied to save the life of a child. So lying isn't so bad after all." "The priest in *Les Miserables* lied by implication when he protected a refugee from the police by stating stolen valuables were gifts. So why can't I protect my friend who just got busted by fabricating an alibi for him?"

A prospective buyer of a few acres of land in Jimison County had several plots under consideration in the western part of the county. Upon examining a spring he noted a greenish deposit that indicated the presence of olivine in the vein of water supplying the spring. "No use looking at the other sites in the county," he said. "I don't want olivine in my water." This man has committed the fallacy of hasty generalization for deposits of olivine in Jimison County are scattered. One spring may be affected and another within three hundred yards may be completely free of the garnet deposits which apparently supply the harmless mineral.

The fallacy of converse accident is represented in the remark, "You saw how that nice young man, John Dean, got fouled up in politics, didn't you? It just goes to show that politics is always a corrupting influence. Politicians are crooked or soon get that way." One who is so cynical about politicians may be thinking of other instances in which politics may have involved corrupt individuals. But to base a universal affirmative proposition on just a few instances is quite unjustified.

A steady, industrious young man, wishing to prepare for the future, entered the stock market. Within a year or so he reported ruefully, "I've quit investing in stocks. Three times I have got enough money ahead to buy a few shares of stock. Each time I studied the companies carefully. Each time the stock went down and has not yet recovered." This young man is generalizing on quite limited experience. He also may have been influenced by a subtle tendency to engage in *post hoc* thinking— after this therefore because of this—to be discussed later in this chapter. He seems to feel that his purchase of stock in a specific company is somehow bad for that company. After he buys

stock the company loses ground and therefore it is because of his investment. It is difficult to see, of course,
how the purchase of stock could be other than helpful to
or good for a company.

The fallacy of converse accident was also committed by
a citizen who was concerned about crime and the difficulties law enforcement officers encounter in apprehend-
ing criminals and in preventing crimes from being committed. He reasoned, "Law enforcement officers have used
court-approved wiretaps to get evidence to convict several
criminals. I think wider, much freer use of wiretaps, even
eliminating 'court-ordered' limitations, is quite in order."

This fallacy is very likely the basis for numerous questionable broad assertions: "All fat people are jolly." "All
Catholics are devout." "All miniature dachshunds make
good pets." "Female physical education majors always
look masculine." "Musicians are temperamental." "Shrinks
themselves are all a bit abaft the beam." "Ministers have a
latent desire to run other people's lives for them." "Only
children are always spoiled." A brief flashing of one's
recollections on the screen of the mind will reveal some
fat acquaintances who are not jolly but are perhaps even
morose; several Catholics who are not very strongly committed to their faith; a petite, feminine physical education
major or two; and so on. And as for only children always
being spoiled, sociological studies have exploded this
myth which probably originated because of hasty generalization.

Proper inductive procedures are a helpful source of information. What is required is either the examination of
a large enough sampling to warrant stating a reasonably
reliable proposition resulting from the examination of the
numerous instances, or a sophisticated, refined method of
selecting a small sampling that will assure a reasonably

reliable generalization about a much larger number of instances.

For example, political polling has become an art in the use of refined inductive procedures. In the early 1930s the *Literary Digest* polled, or conducted what was then called a straw vote among a good many of its subscribers by telephone and predicted a landslide defeat of Franklin D. Roosevelt. Apparently this was not a broad enough sampling. It involved only those financially able to subscribe to a magazine and also to afford telephone service—a fairly limited and select group in that period. The Digest's prediction was in error, as Roosevelt won by a landslide. Contemporary pollsters still use small samples but they try to make sure that their small samples adequately represent a much larger segment of the population.

## 3. COMPOSITION

The fallacy of composition appears to be a close relative of the fallacy of accident. But there is an important difference. The difference is that composition involves a rather fixed unit or organism—a team, a machine, a committee, etc.—while the fallacy of accident involves a quite generalized principle or group. For example, when an alumnus observes that his alma mater's athletic coach has just lined up several all-star football players from several conferences and concludes he's supporting a sure-fire championship team, he may be mistaken. He has committed the fallacy of composition. He has attributed the quality or qualities of several parts of a team to the whole team which is to be made up of those parts. A group of all-stars may not work together smoothly.

A group of musical soloists may produce a terrible quartet, chorus, or chamber orchestra. Similarly, one handy with tools would be foolish to attempt to construct an automobile out of the best individual parts he can find. He may discover that the parts do not fit together. Or, he may discover that one unit of the electrical system cannot be coordinated with another.

Sometimes composition is difficult to distinguish from converse accident, or hasty generalization, because of the difficulty of determining whether one is dealing with a relatively fixed organic unit or a fluid, loosely linked group. Suppose someone says, "Gee, we have an intelligent group of students on our student senate. So we can be sure that they will render sensible judgments." He is committing the fallacy of composition, for a senate, although membership may change considerably, is rather fixed.

But to say, "Our student body is composed of intellectually above average students from all over the state and so the overall average in grades this year will be very high" is to commit the fallacy of converse accident, some will insist. Others will insist this is to commit the fallacy of composition. In any case we should be alert to problems that arise from moving from specifics to generalities or vice versa.

A similar question comes up in regard to the judgment of the sociohistorical analyst, Alexis de Tocqueville, who reasoned that "a majority taken collectively" has the same traits as the individuals composing the majority—their opinions, their interests. "Men," he wrote, "do not change their characters by uniting with each other." Students of group psychology would hardly concur with this assessment.

## 4. DIVISION

The fallacy of division is just the reverse of the fallacy of composition. This fallacy is committed when one moves from the qualities of a unit or whole or organism—a team, machine, committee or the like—to the nature of the individual part or member, applying the qualities of the whole or group to the individual or part involved in the unit or group. So we may repeat in reverse some of the illustrations we have given for the fallacy of composition.

A professional scout who reads the sports pages, notes a championship team and then concludes he will fill his center position on the basketball or football team with the center from the championship team, may not be acting wisely. He would be well advised to study the individual player to see if his own unique qualifications fill the specific needs of the scout's team.

A talent scout who is searching for a soloist for a musical production should not automatically choose a member of a good quartet or chorus without an audition of the individual in question. One may select an automobile of outstanding quality, but he should not expect that each and every individual part will be of comparably high quality when compared with the merit of the entire automobile.

A concerned citizen may extol with justifiable enthusiasm the generally fine legislative body just elected to congress. But he would be misled by the fallacy of division if he were to think that the voting record of any named individual would meet with his equally enthusiastic approval. Foursquare Hospital may have an excellent reputation, one well deserved. But if Yasha Elvitz suspects that he has a serious heart ailment he may, in fact should, explore the merits of Foursquare's cardiac care unit as compared with that of other, possibly less well rated, hospitals before entrusting himself irrevocably to its care. A city may have earned deservedly an award as the Best City in America,

yet a family in transition would do well to see if the basis
of the award included a judgment of the specific things
that family desires most in a city of residence.

Sometimes the fallacy of division is difficult to distinguish from the fallacy of accident just as the fallacy of
composition is difficult to distinguish from the fallacy of
converse accident, and for similar reasons. One must
determine just how fixed the relationship of parts to the
whole may be. In the matter of composition and division
the parts are more inextricably related than is the case
of the parts where accident and converse accident may be
involved.

To clarify the fallacy of division further one additional
illustration may be warranted. "Since the Folksy-wagon is
rated by auto journals as the best foreign car on the market,
its heating system must be tops, too." Since this car, at
least in its earlier models, depends upon an air-cooled
engine, its heating system is notably inefficient in some
respects, defrosting capability for one thing, as compared
with that of many other cars.

## 5. POST HOC FALLACY

The *post hoc* fallacy derives its name from a Latin
expression, *post hoc ergo propter hoc,* "after this therefore
because of this." The fallacy occurs when two events associated in a time sequence are interpreted fallaciously as
having some causal relationship. It is an unfortunate short-
cut in observation of possibly related factors, and it has
been blamed for many of the superstitions we are aware
of linked with the number thirteen, broken mirrors, black
cats, and so on *ad infinitum.* Certainly *post hoc* reasoning
seems sometimes to confirm persons in their superstitions.
One notable example had to do with the launching of
Apollo 13 on a Friday the 13th at 2:13 P.M. Apollo 13 did

have trouble. Therefore those who predicted the venture would be ill fated were able later to say, "I told you so!"

Friends and relatives tried to restrain a pregnant mother from watching a burning house, urging that her baby would be born with a birthmark. Sure enough in the course of time when the baby was born with a rather prominent birthmark on the front of one leg just above the ankle, someone who had been present said, "I told you so! The mother touched her ankle while looking at the boiling smoke and so the baby has a birthmark at that identical spot." The mother protested one detail of the story. She said, "At that time I was so pregnant that it is highly unlikely I touched my ankle."

The study of causal relations is too large an order for development here, but scientists and logicians agree that just because one event follows another in time it does not mean the first event causes the later one. Political history teems with illustrations of how, when a certain person was voted out of office and another in, a war came (or peace came), prosperity developed (or depression ensued), etc. It was only a matter of months after Herbert Hoover and the Republican Party came into power some fifty years ago that our country was in the throes of a depression. "With such evidence as to what a Republican president and his party can cause, you mean to say you're going to vote Republican?"

War and peace and economic changes do not come merely as a result of a single change in an office; the conditions necessary to one or the other are usually a long time in the making. So too with physical and social events. To say that a broken mirror caused a loss in one's stock market holdings ignores the fact that conditions leading to a drop in stock values may have been in the making well before the mirror was broken.

Those who have investigated the development of superstitions sometimes conjecture that superstitions, or at least
many of them, were the fruit of the *post hoc* fallacy: misgivings about broken mirrors, the path of a black cat,
reporting an unhappy dream before breakfast, and many
others. *Post hoc* reasoning, or more specifically the commission of the *post hoc* fallacy, is quite clearly involved in
some short-lived tenets that are akin to superstitions.
Examine the following illustrations.

The clerk in a department store was in a hurry to get to
work, but she had dropped a contact lens and was fran-
tically searching for it. She donned an old Indian necklace
that she had sometimes suggested to friends was a good
luck charm. "Sure enough," she said, "in about three
minutes I located the lens."

As a result of ecology regulations Deam Paper and Fiber
Corporation in Jimison County closed down. For a time
thereafter the seasonal changes in weather seemed to suit
just about everyone in the area. It was no surprise to those
who tune their ears to popular comments to hear several
remarks that went essentially as follows: "See? Didn't I
tell you? Just as soon as Deam Corporation shut down and
reduced their smoke the weather improved. Deam Corporation surely did make bad weather for us." The direct
relation between the paper company's closing and the
clearing of the atmosphere above Jimison County seems
obvious. But the ensuing weeks of irregular weather, ming-
ling bad with good, rather firmly indicated that Jimison
County's weather is not made in Jimison County nor
materially affected by any of its economic enterprises, but
is imported willy nilly from elsewhere.

Sometimes conscience tends not only to make cowards
but to aid and abet in the promotion of the *post hoc* fal-

lacy. At least it was so with the student who bemoaned, "Since I snitched that book from the library I have had difficulty getting down to business with my report. I can't find any of the relevant materials in other books and periodicals while I'm sure there must be plenty. I am becoming convinced that honesty must be a very good policy."

Sports figures are inclined to *post hoc* reasoning. A pitcher will shift his quid to change his luck. A batter will enter the batter's box from only one angle of approach. A coach hopes he will not win the toss in an upcoming game, observing, "So far this season we have lost the toss three times and won every one of those three games. Then last week we won the toss when facing Atlantic Coastal University—and lost that game! No more toss-winning for me, please."

Sometimes the study of logic is successful in relieving one of such bothersome burdens of misgiving. A student volunteered the following. "While in high school I always carried a four-leaf clover with me, especially when faced with tests. I almost always earned A's. After taking a course in logic I quit the practice. I still make A's as often as before. I must have been involved in a *post hoc* fallacy."

Causal relations are so involved with various fallacies and especially the *post hoc* fallacy as to prompt the inclusion of a discussion of causal analysis in the appendix. Those who wish to do so may turn to that analysis before proceeding with other fallacies involving the omission of relevant data.

## 6. Special Pleading

The fallacy of special pleading occurs when someone, because of subjective limitations produced by his own personal concerns or by deliberate intent, presents only one side of a case, the one favorable to him. A person with vested interests, whether a large stockholder in a corporation or the owner of a humble home, is most likely to yield to this fallacy.

Let us say a question has arisen as to the location of a highway. An owner of a company with road building contracts may support a particular route because of the profit to be realized. He supports a scenic route knowing it will be more expensive, but he stresses the scenery anyway. A homeowner along this route may vote with him, if his, the homeowner's, property value will be improved, or he may vote against him if his property value will be depreciated.

The annals of business and politics and especially lobbying are well filled with illustrations of special pleading. Boyd Whimsdale, a member of the board of county commissioners in Hinterland County, is a most ardent advocate of establishing a racetrack in the county. It happens that Whimsdale owns a chain of motels in the surrounding tourist area. It is difficult to erase the notion that some special pleading is involved in his urging that the track will be advantageous financially and otherwise to many citizens of the county.

In any national election year, appeals for votes are borne on promises that reveal special pleading if examined closely. A congressman from an area where taxation is a concern of voters will promise to reduce taxes without noting that government services must be curtailed or the national debt ceiling must be raised if taxes are reduced. Another congressman from an area supported extensively by defense contracts will vigorously advocate a heavy defense department budget but will mention briefly if at all the necessity of raising taxes or moving the country further into debt if defense expenditures continue high or are increased.

Loan companies issue appeals to those burdened by a variety of debts to combine their obligations into one so that they may write only one check each month. The companies are careful to avoid mention of the possibility that their interest rates may be higher than the interest involved in the varied debts that are to be combined.

It is a rather generally accepted practice for lawyers, whether involved in civil or criminal cases, to present only evidence that is favorable to their clients. But it becomes the responsibility of the judge, jury or opposing lawyer to watch for omitted points to round out efforts to get at the whole truth.

## 7. Oversimplification

Brevity may be the soul of wit but it is not necessarily the soul of rational wisdom. William of Ockham introduced a valid and tremendously important principle when he said that to get at truth one must shave off all superfluities. According to his principle, usually termed "Ockham's Razor," the simplest explanation is the correct one. But we are concerned here with shaving off too much—with *over* simplifying.

"High prices are the result of wage increases," "One atomic bomb on Hanoi would have put a prompt end to our problems in Southeast Asia," or "All we need to do to straighten out our country is to return to the faith of our fathers" are apt illustrations of oversimplification. Wage increases are only one factor in bringing about high prices. One atomic bomb on Hanoi might have put a prompt end to Hanoi but how could that have solved all of our problems in relation to the southeastern parts of Asia? To the faith of which of our fathers should we return? That of

Jefferson or Jefferson's critics? That of the Puritans or that of the Virginia cavaliers? And even if we could agree upon which fathers, would one simple creed resolve the complex problems of today, when some of our developments were not envisioned by any of our fathers?

In the course of the energy crisis of 1974 one proposal for dealing with the oil producing and exporting countries went along lines like this: "All we have to do is to find a way to take over one strategic bit of land in the oil producing countries—by purchase, by lease for ninety-nine years, or by finding some treaty loophole that will allow us to station troops there. We won't find those people acting up any more." In one fell swoop we have here offered three overly simplified choices.

Many products are offered with the alluring promise of simplicity, variations on the theme developed by an enterprising advertising copywriter for an electronics company: "If you can use a small screwdriver, a pair of sharpnosed pliers and an electric soldering iron then you can build your very own color television set worth at least $600. And you can do it from our $189 television kit." Producers of motorboats and sailboats, grandfather clocks, furniture, and innumerable other complicated items promise similar beguiling ease in assembling your own fine finished products.

Traditional sayings, proverbs, aphorisms and slogans, discussed in some detail elsewhere, are types of over-simplification. "Spare the rod and spoil the child" implies that all that is needed for proper child development is the generous use of corporal punishment. "Reading maketh a full man." Not necessarily if it is repetitious or if it is trivial. A perceptive teen-ager declined to respond to an altar call at an evangelistic meeting saying, "I don't believe it is quite as simple as that."

## 8. BLACK-OR-WHITE

As a label for a fallacy in logic "black-or-white" derives from the figurative expression, "He sees only in black or white, never in shades of gray." Sometimes this is termed "false dilemma." Some, however, object to the latter term for while etymologically "dilemma" means the presentation of "two assumptions" the word has come to mean somewhat more commonly the presentation of two choices neither of which is particularly attractive to the one who must make a choice. This use of the term will be examined in a later chapter.

"He that is not for us is against us" is a statement in black-or-white thinking for it admits of no other possibility, neutrality, for example. "We must win or lose" omits the possibility that, let us say, in a game a tie is possible.

A bumper sticker bears the exhortation "Get your (picture of a heart) in Dixie or get your (picture of a donkey—an ass) out." Such a demand would appear to be an emotional reaction against proposals to change some of the restrictive laws and practices of the southland. It gives wide berth to the possibility—even likelihood—that one who seeks what he believes to be constructive changes has his heart, figuratively speaking, very much in Dixie.

Analysis of the black-or-white fallacy follows very appropriately the discussion of oversimplification for it is a form of oversimplification. Human resourcefulness is such that one should not find it too heavy a task to examine proposals of simple, limited alternatives to discover whether or not there are still other possibilities for decision or action.

## 9. ARGUMENT OF THE BEARD

Superficially the argument of the beard may appear to be the black-or-white fallacy in a flimsy disguise. But the two are not to be confused. While the black-or-white argument proposes only two alternatives, the argument of the beard proposes far too many possibilities. The term, argument of the beard, comes from the old, old quibble as to how many whiskers it takes to make a beard. One seems to be too few. Two, 3, or even 4 seem to be too few. But 101? 302? 789? 1,000? At what number does a bunch of whiskers deserve the label "beard"?

Two friends were leaving the gymnasium after a workout at handball and it was a Friday afternoon. One suddenly remembered he had left his watch and started back to get it. His companion asked, "Let's see now. We've been gone only five minutes. Do you suppose it's still there?" "Yes, I would imagine so." "Reckon it will be there fifteen minutes from now?" "Yes, very likely." "Three hours from now? Tomorrow? Sunday? Why not wait until our game Monday afternoon? By your own reasoning your watch is safe."

A prominent physicist reasoned this way to justify leaving small children alone so he and his wife could join friends across town for an evening of bridge. Whether he ever acted on the basis of such reasoning he does not say. Presumably he was being facetious. At any rate his children are now grown.

Instructors rather regularly have difficulty at registration time with student appeals like this: "I know the seats assigned for Philosophy 2360 are all filled. But one more will not really matter. I'll bring in an extra chair. Please admit me."

Those following the argument of the beard type of thinking reason that one more chocolate cream won't affect your weight much, that one more day of smoking won't produce cancer, or that using company postage won't affect the balance sheet adversely. Where are lines to be drawn?

Before moving on to exercises let us return to the illustrations of fallacies introducing this chapter. Their nature should now be readily recognizable.

The critic of welfare has committed the fallacy of converse accident. He has generalized all too hastily if his comments represent all the examination he has made of the subject of welfare. He has omitted a great deal of data, some of which might support his position and some of which might give him pause in his judgment.

According to the tourists' reports, those abroad who think any individual American is wealthy is committing either the fallacy of accident, misapplying a generalization, or the fallacy of division, applying a characteristic of a country as a whole to one of its component parts, a citizen.

Blaming a series of events (in the case of the illustration given, wars) upon their being merely sequential in relation to other events is a commission of the *post hoc* fallacy.

### EXERCISES: CHAPTER 3

Label the following according to the fallacy each most aptly illustrates.

1. "Each member of President Washington's cabinet was a very capable man. We can be assured, therefore, that the cabinet was very capable."
2. "Perhaps high prices and less food intake will be good for our health. Look at the Watsusis who eat so little, especially rich foods. Few of them have heart attacks."
3. "This formula is made from six prescription-type ingredients."
4. The trustees of Upstate University were troubled by a falling off in enrollments. The chairman proposed, "What we need to do is to replace the director of

admissions. Some new blood in that office and we will see enrollments pick up."

5. "Vote for Soundoff for the Senate for his second term. Remember? Within two weeks of his first election, federal funds coming into our state nearly doubled!"

6. "In this course you students will either get an A or an F. Either you know the material or you don't!"

7. "I have taken an abstinence pledge, for alcohol has been shown to wreak so much havoc on individuals and on society. So doc will just have to prescribe something else than beer for my urological problem."

8. "Our country! Love it or leave it."

9. "They must certainly be the most permissive parents around."
   "Why so?"
   "Didn't you see how promptly they said yes when Rollo asked if he could use the car tonight?"

10. "The Federal Government is notably inefficient in its work, and in its business affairs specifically. When I was an administrator with the Upstate Life and Casualty Company we wouldn't hire anyone who had had a turn in government service."

11. Mother, trying to calm worried father: "Even if they were out until past three, what of it? Her date comes from a fine family, and she and he wouldn't be doing anything out of line."

12. "My doctor said I should take a stiff drink or two each night to dilate my capillaries and relieve high blood pressure. So I am recommending a couple of good nightcaps for all my friends whose blood pressure is up."

13. A recent president vetoed health appropriations on the grounds that they were inflationary. He did not

weigh, at least for the public, the fact that six health centers for veterans, prison inmates and the destitute would be closed, and that cancer research at one center would be set back for a year. Nor did he indicate any consideration had been given to closing out other quite questionable governmental programs instead.

14. "Looks like we must either underwrite grain sales and put up with inflation to keep the Russians friendly, or let them go hungry and hate us while we bask in our own plenty."

15. "All of the members of that church are wealthy so the church must also be wealthy."

16. "That's a very successful brokerage firm so their representative, Simpkins, is sure to guide me to a money-making stock."

17. "There is one sure way to turn students into thinkers: require that they take a course in logic."

18. "I wouldn't think of starting a trip of any consequence without having my house in apple pie order. I call it 'dying shape.' I'm sure if I left it in a mess I would have a serious accident. So cleaning up helps keep me safe."

19. A proponent of the use of LSD argued that the aging process destroys brain cells so that one has fewer at forty years of age than at twenty-five, say, fewer still at fifty, sixty, and so on. Therefore, he concluded the use of LSD, which is believed to destroy brain cells, is not so bad since they are going to be destroyed gradually anyway.

20. "Better dead than Red, and what other choice is there?"

21. The president of a large corporation recently advanced

the view that the more money he personally makes the better it is for his company and for the people of the country.

22. "I know there is an energy crisis, including a shortage of electric power in some areas. But does that mean a dam must be built to flood our lovely valley, covering ten homesites and a cemetery? Certainly we can find alternatives to such a plan."

23. A trout fisherman had caught one more trout than the legal limit and pled with the warden: "After all, I'm from out of state and the license cost me twenty bucks. I ought to be entitled to just one more little old fish. Surely there are plenty of them left and there'll be more when the stream is restocked."

24. "Welfare programs should be abolished. News reports in the last week have carried reports of three people collecting welfare checks and buying food stamps illegally. There's widespread corruption and waste in the system."

25. A zealous young minister recently persuaded a group of young people to burn a number of musical tapes and recordings. He reported that interviews of 1000 persons had revealed that 984 of them had engaged in fornication while listening to the kind of music involved.

## COMMENTS ON EXERCISES FOR CHAPTER 3

1. Composition.
2. Converse accident or hasty generalization. This fallacy could also result from *post hoc* reasoning or over-simplification.
3. Composition. Some of the ingredients might cancel out the good effects of other ingredients or combine with them to produce undesirable side effects.

4. Oversimplification. There could be unusual situations in which a singularly ineffective person's replacement would boost enrollments in a college. But more often than not other measures would be necessary.

5. *Post hoc.* Certainly the senator's booster or his audience should examine whether or not the federal funds resulted from his predecessor's work rather than from Soundoff's efforts.

6. The black-or-white fallacy.

7. Accident. The fellow in urological distress seems to be sticking too rigorously to a general principle, making no exception for medical reasons.

8. Black-or-white. There are other possible modes of action. A critic of his country may love it so he wishes to improve it. He could, of course, love it and leave it to advertise it abroad, promote business relations, or for other reasons.

9. Hasty generalization.

10. Division, attributing qualities of the whole to one of its (in this case former) parts.

11. Division. The mother's reaction could be construed as the *ad hominem* fallacy.

12. A bit of reasoning involving hasty generalization. While alcohol may relieve high blood pressure in one person, it might aggravate the condition in another type of person.

13. Special pleading.

14. Black-or-white.

15. Composition.

16. Division.

17. Oversimplification.

18. *Post hoc.*

19. Argument of the beard.

20. Black-or-white.

21. What the fallacy is in the "trickle down theory" could
    be debated. Of the fallacies discussed in this chapter
    it would represent the fallacy of composition—what
    is good for any citizen is good for the entire popu-
    lation. There is an implicit notion, perhaps, of special
    pleading and rationalization.
22. Special pleading.
23. Argument of the beard, and an appeal to sympathy.
24. Converse accident.
25. *Post hoc.*

# Chapter 4

# Pseudo-Evidence

As we see from the preceding chapters there are a good many ways of falling short of the human potential for rationality. There is misusing and sometimes abusing of language. There is much diverting of attention from or digressing from issues. There is deliberate and inadvertent omitting of data which should be recognized as relevant to issues at hand. But those types of poor thinking or argumentation do not by any means cover all possible faults.

From time to time we offer or are offered data or evidence which is not data or evidence at all. It is material that is merely paraded as evidence, material that will not bear careful scrutiny.

"This law has been on the books of this state for nearly one hundred years," proclaimed a state legislator. "This should be reason enough for letting it remain intact. But more than that it embodies a principle that the great

economist Adam Smith espoused in his *Wealth of Nations.*
And just a few years ago this law was upheld in a decision
by that great jurist, Judge Hayneston."

"No, I'm not interested in shifting any of my savings to
any type of investment no matter how good it looks. 'A bird
in the hand is worth two in the bush,' I always say."

Rejection for admission to a club brings a somewhat
common response. "After all, the members of that club are
a rather snobbish group and I can certainly find better
ways to spend my time and money than in their often inane
activities. I wasn't very interested anyway."

A presidential candidate practically shouts, "Polls? Who
cares about polls? I tell you that come the primaries I'll be
ahead, and that's what counts. I guarantee you I'll get the
votes!"

These and other forms pseudo-evidence takes are the
focus of the following several pages.

### 1. MISUSE OF AUTHORITY, OR ARGUMENTUM AD VERECUNDIAM

Life is sufficiently complex that we must depend upon
authorities in many areas. We need a medical doctor to
diagnose physical ailments. We need a repairman to put a
television set in order. We need an architect to design a
house or determine the weight a bridge can stand.

But we misuse authorities when we associate them with
something out of their field—our reverence or respect for
a person thus misleads us. When a doctor recommends,
personally or in an advertisement, a particular kind of
television set, we should not let his testimonial weigh
heavily. When a television repairman recommends a certain kind of laxative and his advice is accepted the one
suffering from irregularity is misusing an authority.

While in a democracy all citizens must decide upon certain kinds of legislation, one does not follow the counsel

of an architect regarding, say, school systems, without ascertaining whether or not he also has some competence in the area of education. When we buy a cosmetic because it is associated in an advertisement with a movie star, or use a razor recommended by an athlete, or drink a brand of beer because oil prospectors celebrate a strike with that particular beverage, we are misusing authorities in the sense that we are associating ideas which are not logically related.

Misuse of authority or appeal to reverence (which is what *argumentum ad verecundiam* means) sometimes applies to other things than individuals. When the legislator argued against amending a state constitution simply because the section at issue for deletion is over a hundred years old, he is appealing to reverence for antiquity or age. When an advertisement pictures a soaring eagle to promote some product which has no connection whatever with bird-life the purpose is to develop what is sometimes called "meaning from association"—a variation on the appeal to reverence.

There are those who "reason" in terms of the dear little old lady in the advertisement which capitalizes on our American tendency to appreciate dear little old ladies and the traditional postman. The lady admires the postman and says, "Our postman is in fine physical condition. This morning he told me he goes right for Cofbane for his nagging cough when he gets a cold, which he rarely does. So I'm heading right to the drug store for some Cofbane now."

Well-known figures are so appealing that their judgments are sometimes unquestioned. "The messages of the prophets, Gibbon's story of the fall of Rome and Billy Graham's sermons all warn of doom for the nation. There's nothing anyone, I least of all, can do. Ruin is inevitable." Were not the prophets ethically responsible men speaking to the problems of their times, rather than to nations twenty-five hundred or more years distant from them? However competent Gibbon's historical analysis was, does it necessarily mean his observations are proper, fixed guides now? And Billy Graham would deliberately take us back to the prophets of old as a basis for our judgments.

Historically prominent figures are rung in time and time again with little care as to the respective contexts in which they spoke and those in which they are cited. "We are more and more involved in foreign alliances. Have we completely forgotten the warning of George Washington that we should avoid foreign entanglements?" "Vote Republican. It is the great historic party of Abraham Lincoln." "Vote Democratic. Our heritage is that of Thomas Jefferson."

Sometimes the use of authority as a basis of appeal goes awry—but only with those that have retentive memories. An alcoholic beverage depicts Babe Ruth in an advertisement in a posture indicating he has hit a good one, possibly another home run. A picture of a bottle of the beverage takes up nearly half the page bearing the Babe's likeness. The implication seems to be that the Sultan of Swat enjoyed the specific beverage, Olde Slam Bam. But, alas, if he did enjoy it he enjoyed it overmuch. He is reported to have had a problem with alcohol to the extent that it affected his baseball performance adversely, as great as his overall record was.

The misuse of authority or the presenting of pleasant associations with products, however farfetched the associations, is extensive. Tennis players endorse toothpaste. A professional football star dons ladies' hose for a photograph. A leading stunt driver gives a testimonial that he prefers a Divalvi for stunts and therefore it would make a tough, safe and efficient family car.

Mythical figures get in on the act as when Santa Claus

displays a portable computer saying, "If it's the thought that counts, give the one that counts best." This is a triple threat fallacy combining the Santa Claus appeal, equivocation on the word "counts," and the dogmatic assertion that this computer is better than any other.

It is certainly to be hoped that the legislation proposed to assure more responsibly informative advertising when prominent figures are involved will be enacted. It would also be helpful if someone could come up with a way to eliminate irrelevant associations from advertising. We must remember, though, that while various types of advertising media are so painfully prominent in their abuse in this regard, others than promoters of business who have an idea to sell are also guilty of misuse of authorities.

## 2. DOGMATIC MANNER

When we accept a proposition with no supporting evidence largely because the speaker or writer asserts it very forcefully, we are falling victim to the dogmatic manner or the confident assertion. Politicians, who seem gifted at a variety of indiscretions in logic, are particularly prone to make dogmatic statements. "When I take my seat in the state senate . . ." "Even if the news media is against us we will win by a landslide!"

Advertisers share this aptness with politicians. "No fibers can approach ours in durability, texture, and color." "We guarantee you more mileage than with any other car." Occasionally an advertiser unwittingly reveals that beneath his confident manner lurk some reservations. A case in point is that of the razor company that boasts, "A dollar says you can't match our razor in smooth shaving." Are they willing to gamble only a paltry dollar?

"If you want the best cavity fighter use tingly Tasti-Dent." "Try the most delicious homemade dinner made in a restaurant." Note also the internal inconsistency, or contradictory terms "homemade" and "made in a restaurant," a type of fallacy to be discussed in the following chapter. "To get the longest eyelashes ever, use Amaze-aline." "If you once use our recording tape you will never use another brand." "This is the most delicious, alluring fragrance of any perfume in the world." By whose sense of smell or by whose psychological association with varying odors?

News analysts as well as politicians and advertisers issue pronouncements very confidently which they do not support adequately and which their readers usually have no means of verifying. "Golda Meir and Mosha Dayan most certainly agree that this line must remain drawn as it now stands." "Under the surface of apparent discord between Russian and China, Communism most surely remains monolithic." No doubt many a news reporter is being honest in making assertions without mentioning reliable sources which he might have cited. But many a time it is well to hold such unsupported assertions suspect.

Psychology and logic converge at many points and centering on the dogmatically inclined person is one such case. When a stand-up comic says, "This is true," expect a piece of bizarre fiction. Common introductory phrases like the following should arouse at least a little suspicion that something questionable or at least exaggerated is about to come forth. "I promise." "I swear." "Cross my heart." "I'm going to level with you." Beware when one of the following is tacked on to a rather positive statement. "You better believe it." "Believe you me." "Now, that's the gospel truth."

### 3. APHORISM CITING, OR CLICHÉ USAGE

Aphorism citing and the use of clichés are in some respects like the appeal to reverence for authorities for they are a resort to a proverb, aphorism, slogan or very familiar phrase. Some have been voiced by an alleged sage. Others have simply grown familiar and respected through frequent usage and recurring articulation.

"Early to bed and early to rise makes a man healthy, wealthy and wise" is an oft quoted proverb but a gross oversimplification. It requires much more than such a sleep schedule to maintain good health, acquire riches, and develop wisdom.

An adult, and especially the elderly, may decline to undertake a new study or adopt a potentially useful gadget because "You can't teach an old dog new tricks." Even if it is true that old dogs are difficult to teach new tricks, there is considerable evidence that there are other factors than just age that determine a human being's capacity to learn. Continuing education classes enroll a great many adults, including senior citizens, who derive pleasure and benefit from learning new tricks.

A few excerpts from a potentially large catalog of aphorisms and clichés are these. "Get out the vote. As Lincoln said, 'The ballot is stronger than the bullet.' " "You can't beat the system." "If you can't stand the heat, get out of the kitchen." "Better late than never." (With some clever rejoinders it is "Better never than late.") "When the going gets tough the tough get going."

The contradictions in many aphorisms should alert us to their questionable nature: "Look before you leap" versus "He who hesitates is lost." "A rolling stone gathers no moss" versus "Travel broadens one." "A bird in the hand is worth two in the bush" versus "Nothing ventured nothing gained." "All work and no play makes Jack a dull boy" versus "Better to wear out than rust out."

Those under thirty may be less cliché ridden than their elders for they do not seem to have been required to memorize excerpts from *Poor Richard's Almanac,* McGuffey's

*Reader* or the Book of Proverbs. But they tend to develop their own clichés. "Never trust anyone over thirty." "If it feels good, do it." "Let it all hang out." "Turn on, tune in and drop out."

## 4. RATIONALIZING

It can be debated as to whether rationalizing falls within the scope of logic or more properly in the area of psychology. But since certain other fallacies result from one's own slant and are therefore corrected only by practicing psychological discipline, and since we are concerned with raising caution signs, we will also examine rationalizing.

Rationalizing is the procedure whereby one justifies a position on the basis of a reason that he offers instead of a frank appraisal of his real reason or reasons. In rationalizing, one must first of all ignore principles of logic which he may otherwise recognize. But the results of adopting clear facts and relating them logically yields conclusions he does not relish. So he supplants these with propositions more palatable to him.

A student may persuade his advisor to endorse the dropping of a course by insisting that he can do more thorough work and earn better grades if he is carrying fewer credit hours. Actually, he has just pledged a fraternity and initiation assignments promise him a more busy and exciting life than poring over books.

A student may wish to attend a popular but not particularly worthwhile movie and so, rationalizing, advance the argument of the beard. "Putting off studying one more night won't hurt." He may even toss in a cliché for good measure. "An evening of fun never hurts anyone."

Rationalizing may be used to justify failure. In the classic fable of the fox unable to reach the attractive bunch of grapes, the fox opines, "They are sour anyway." A variation of this has come into use in recent years as when one justifies a poor choice he has made through the "sweet lemon" device. For example, an affluent friend bought a luxury car which cost so much he was reluctant to reveal the figure. He went into great detail about the merits of the basic elements of the car and the optional equipment with which it was heavily laden. Later it developed he was emphasizing certain factors because he was sadly disappointed in some of the serious deficiencies in the car.

A well-worn illustration of rationalization is the situation in which a girl who does not get asked to be a date for a dance says, "I didn't really want to go anyway. The Humper Bumpers is not a good band and dances here are always a drag anyhow."

A couple of further illustrations are these. A young man had his motorcycle stolen due to his own negligence. He said, "Oh well. If I still had it I would have to shell out fifty or sixty bucks just to get it running again and no telling how much to keep it in shape. It's just as well the damned thing is gone." A man was approached for a pledge for the United Fund. He responded, "I give to charities the old, hard way, selecting individual projects. The United Fund supports things like Little League Baseball, scouting, and so on that I think ought to be financed by parents of the children involved or by merchants. And I believe the United Fund overhead is excessive." He may be rationalizing.

Returning to the illustrations early in this chapter, the first illustrates misuse of authority in advancing the thought of one economist from decades ago, one judge, and the longevity of the statute. The second cites a cliché or proverb. The third example about the rejected club aspirant involves rationalization. And the presidential candidate is trying to buoy up spirits by his confident manner and dogmatic assertions.

## EXERCISES: CHAPTER 4

Label the following according to the fallacy each most aptly illustrates.

1. "Don't be so apprehensive about getting busted. 'Every cloud has a silver lining.' Something good is bound to come out of it."

2. David Hume, philosophical epitome of skepticism, defended a position he was advancing by saying, "I appeal to a man celebrated for piety and philosophy. It is Father Malebranche."

3. "I have just been reading Freud's *Future of an Illusion,* and he clearly says that educated men today must find religious belief impossible."

4. "I didn't want that job anyway. That outfit is hard to work for, pays low wages, and promotes mighty slowly."

5. "The longer it's aged the better!"

6. "There were two doctors and three interns in that TV play. Did you notice that at staff meetings everyone smoked cigarettes? So cigarettes must not be bad for you."

7. Smogley does not like his instructor because the course is difficult. The reasons he gives for wanting to drop the course are that the instructor speaks so slowly and carefully as to be boring, that he is a walking encyclopedia of useless facts, and that he nitpicks over errors in students' papers.

8. "This knife will make other knives you use instantly obsolete."

9. Martin Luther responded to Copernicus' proposal for revisions in the theory of celestial motion by directing people's attention to the story of Joshua's command to the sun to stand still, which indirectly proved, he claimed, as a biblical report, that the sun moved about the earth.

10. "You are mighty right I go to church. I was in the service in Korea and again in Vietnam, and you know there are no atheists in foxholes!"

11. Galileo argued that air—and all the elements except fire—had weight. He based his argument upon Aristotle's claim that this is the case.

12. Student planning a week-end jaunt: "I don't know why I should stay and study. These requirements for graduation are stupid. And this crop of profs I've got is from Dullsville. Besides, social development is mighty important, you know."

13. "You ought to get one of these attachments for your carburetor."
    "I think it costs too much."
    "So you're going to be penny wise and pound foolish, are you?"

14. "All we have to fear is fear itself."

15. "Now, I'll just take in the movie. And if I get called on in class tomorrow I'll just explain that the movie, billed as entertainment, was really an artistic production good for my cultural development."

16. The promoters of an alcoholic beverage boast that it was the Scotch of Henry VIII.

17. "Sure I use a hairbrush sometimes on the kids. 'Spare the rod and spoil the child!' "

18. An advertisement of a manual on investments reads, "How to beat the depression that is surely coming. Tested techniques to help you weather the coming

financial storm and make money out of it besides."
19. "Sure, I eat an apple in some form every day, even if it's only in apple pie. 'An apple a day keeps the doctor away,' I've always heard."
20. "Feed a cold and starve a fever. Starve a cold and start a fever."

## Comments on Exercises for Chapter 4

1. Aphorism citing or cliché usage. Many clichés also involve, as this one does, the misuse of analogy, to be discussed in the next chapter. Even if every large condensation of moisture were to have a silvery top side, which is not the case, a psychological, emotional or legal cloud is still a very different matter.
2. Misuse of authority. Father Malebranche was a priest and more of a theologian than a philosopher and it is curious that the skeptic Hume deigned to quote him.
3. Misuse of authority. Freud was a psychologist and not a theologian nor a philosopher in the restricted sense of those terms. Moreover, Freud may be somewhat suspect for engaging in circular reasoning in this instance, that is, he may think, "If a man is educated, he will not hold religious beliefs. And if he holds religious beliefs, he is not educated."
4. Rationalization.
5. Dogmatic manner.
6. Misuse of authority.
7. Rationalization.
8. Dogmatic manner.
9. Misuse of authority.
10. Cliché usage.
11. Misuse of authority. Aristotle deserves much credit for his philosophical inquiries and he engaged in

near-scientific investigations. But during the post-Medieval period he was used much too widely as an authority. Thinkers referred to him instead of utilizing and refining his methods of inquiry.

12. Rationalization.
13. Cliché usage.
14. Dogmatic manner involving a bit of circular thinking.
15. Rationalization.
16. Misuse of authority. This would be a curious advertisement in the light of some of the physiological distress of Henry's later years.
17. Cliché usage.
18. Dogmatic manner.
19. Cliché usage.
20. Cliché usage. Is it quoted correctly, or should it be reversed? Some clichés, especially those involving mnemonic devices, are best left alone.

# Chapter 5

# Misleading Presumptions

Ours is a generation confident that its choices are by and large underwritten by evidence that would be convincing to the proverbial man from Missouri. Immersed in the marvels of science and technology we are smug in the notion that it is difficult for anyone to sell us an undesirable bill of goods. Our very smugness may make us unwary. We at times may be bemused by assertions that seem, but only seem, to imply sound evidence. All too often assertions that are casually persuasive prove upon careful analysis to claim more than they warrant.

A columnist representing a conservative organization urged that government regulation of business be completely eliminated. "For government to regulate business in any way," he wrote, "is like having a manager of a professional ball team serve as referee in a game the team is playing. Or, worse still, it makes the government both judge and jury as to how business practices should be handled."

A psychic healer reasoned somewhat like certain religious faith healers when he said to a subject, "The reason you are not responding to treatment of your migraine headaches is that you are not concentrating on sending out the right brain waves. If you would only let go and send out the right waves you would never have migraine again. But since you are still complaining of headaches it must be because you are not following my instructions."

"It appears we may have been on the wrong side when we got involved in both world wars," complains a prominent political aspirant. "If we had not fought the Kaiser, communism would never have got off the ground as a political force. But we fought the Kaiser and communism got a start. And again we did it wrong. If we had stayed out of World War II, other nations would have worn themselves out, and we would clearly be having our own way in establishing world peace and harmony."

These and several other types of arguments related to them are faulty in that they seem to imply more than they really do, logically speaking.

We cannot always blame the other fellow for misleading us with superfluous or inappropriate implications. We will fall into the same errors from time to time in trying to think through problems, especially when we become aggressive in attempting to persuade others to our point of view. Here are five slightly different ways in which this may happen.

## 1. MISUSE OF ANALOGY

Analogies are very useful. They may have been the basis for much of man's development of knowledge. Certainly as man progressed into the scientific era he found analogies to be helpful in discovery and invention. One of the earliest reports of a discovery made by the use of analogy was Archimedes' solution of the problem the king had posed for him. The well-known problem was how to determine whether the proper amount of gold had been used in making the king's crown. An overflowing tub of water prompted Archimedes' insight into the principle of displacement.

Teachers find analogies extremely useful in instruction. Releasing an inflated toy balloon to swirl through the air, for instance, demonstrates aptly the principle of jet propulsion. Playing a game of pop the whip can demonstrate very vividly some principles involved in the motion of a wheel.

We extend our own personal knowledge time after time by analogical thinking. A screw with a Phillips head is loose and in a position where the Phillips screwdrivers at hand are too long to get at it for tightening. Remembering that a large nail is pointed like such a screwdriver one may bend the point of the nail a quarter of an inch or so from the end, insert it and—presto—a tightened screw.

However, analogies must be used carefully and with due regard to the differences between things being compared. When an advertisement states that just as charcoal filtering gives a better tasting drink of water so too will a charcoal filter give a better tasting cigarette, we have reason to wonder. We want water to be virtually tasteless, and charcoal helps eliminate substances having inappropriate taste. But do we want a cigarette to be similarly nearly tasteless?

An opponent of the public financing of national political campaigns argues that a law limiting what a candidate can spend on a campaign is the same as a law limiting a speech to ten minutes. The differences between the two are obvious, but one has misgivings that all too few who heard the analogy recognized the fallacy involved.

An advocate of the use of LSD said that if the drug is to continue to be outlawed then fire and water should be outlawed too. All three, he insisted, are dangerous in the wrong hands, in massive quantities or used at the wrong time or place. We do not need firsthand knowledge of the effects of LSD to spot the faults in this analogy.

Here are a number of analogies which merit some logical analysis. An advocate of college courses on marriage and family living recommends that just as one visits his dentist and doctor annually for examinations, so too should he visit a counselor to analyze his family situation at regular intervals. A different but equally inappropriate analogy would recommend against such counseling. Digging a plant up from time to time to examine its roots will stunt or kill the plant. Looking at a marriage and family situation from time to time is likely to cause it irreparable damage. The counselor referred to earlier further suggested that just as a tooth or an appendix sometimes needs to be removed, so a divorce is sometimes necessary. This is an absurd comparison indeed.

An advocate of greatly increased national armaments responded to a criticism in the following manner. "Our good friend argues that building more missile sites, atomic submarines and modernized bombers will inevitably lead to war. Would he say, then, that building more fire stations would lead to more fires? That setting up more medical clinics would lead to more disease?" There are marked differences between fire stations and medical clinics and tools of destruction. One important distinction is that the fire stations and medical clinics threaten no one and give comfort in a feeling of security. We would certainly not compare an unfriendly country's development of arms to its development of fire stations and medical clinics!

An antitobacconist proposes heavy taxes on tobacco products, affirming that we ought to "fight fire with fire." The aim of the antitobacconist may be a worthy one, but the analogy is inept. A meat wholesaler suggests that having half a steer in one's freezer is like having money in the bank. Certainly it is good to have meat on hand. But do not expect it to accrue interest. Rather hope it will not, for if the meat "accrues interest" it may become unfit to eat.

Here are some more questionable analogies. "Foods need 'Accentuate' like flowers need water." "Poetry is a game with words just as football is a game with a ball." "The development of Russia is like the growth of a person: one day a toddler and the next an adult with no adolescence between."

Anthologies of old quotations are replete with analogies that will not bear critical analysis. Variously attributed to William Penn, Benjamin Franklin, and possibly others is the saying, "Justice is the insurance we have on our lives and obedience is the premium we pay for it." Others from an anthology: "Minds are like parachutes. They function only when open." "Human minds are like wagons. When they have a light load they are much noisier than when the load is heavy." Mark Twain is said to have complained that since writing and speaking were his trades, it was no more fair to ask him for a free sample thereof than to ask a doctor for a corpse.

## 2. INTERNAL INCONSISTENCIES, OR CONTRADICTORY TERMS

The fallacy of internal inconsistency occurs when one includes in a sentence words that contradict each other or states propositions in which the terms stand in stark conflict. A song that enjoyed a period of popularity was one in which the singer aspired to dream an impossible dream. One might dream a highly improbable dream but it is extending poetic license to have one dreaming an impossible dream.

A sign in a shop boasts, "The Difficult Task We Do Immediately. The Impossible Takes Us a Bit Longer." This is an amusing sign but, taken literally, is nonsense. The claim is internally inconsistent.

The following is an illustration either of inherently contradictory statements or euphemistic language or possibly both. A public official was under fire for belonging to an exclusive club which had rejected a Black who had applied for membership. His response was this: "We didn't turn him down. We simply didn't accept him."

Similar but much more tragic situations are represented in these inconsistencies: the officer in Vietnam who said as he touched a lighter to a thatched hut, "We must destroy this village in order to save it," and Yasir Arafat's contention, "We do not want to destroy anyone. It is precisely because we have been advocating coexistence that we have shed so much blood."

Some internal inconsistencies are word tangles we inflict upon ourselves. Such is the old problem, "What happens when an irresistible force meets an immovable object?" Since irresistible forces and immovable objects are defined in terms of each other, they have no business being incorporated into such a question as this.

Some inconsistencies are amusing, but they may cause problems. Such was the U. S. Post Office memorandum which announced service awards for men who die before retirement, but which had to be requested three weeks prior to death! Another was the report of a study of a particular police system in which records showed that assaults by citizens upon policemen had decreased one hundred and fifty percent within a year. This, it was held, showed promise of further decreases. How can anything decrease more than one hundred percent?

The following are illustrations of statements or coupled propositions that involve readily apparent internal contradictions. An automobile advertisement uses the pitch:

"This isn't the time to buy a big car. This isn't the time to buy a small car. Now is the time to buy a single car that's both." An instructor in backpacking procedures said, "The best kind of warm, comfortable sock is one made of twenty-five percent cotton and one hundred percent wool." A zipper advertisement questions, "Why is our invisible zipper more invisible than theirs?" An astronomy instructor directed his students, "Look very carefully at the rings around Saturn and you can almost see an invisible line at the point we are talking about." A movie starlet confessed, "I have an unconscious devotion to the first fellow I ever dated steadily." A frequent compliment is paid atomic physicists for "Doing the impossible, splitting the atom."

Occasionally an internally inconsistent statement is so descriptive that one might prefer to let it stand unchallenged. Such was the observation of a weary committee member who observed after a long and wearying debate over a very minor item, "Our discussion has reached a point of monumental insignificance."

One of the most curious contentions regarding reason in the handling of facts was that of Beaumarchais in *Barbier de Seville:* "It is not necessary to retain facts that we may reason concerning them."

### 3. HYPOTHESIS CONTRARY TO FACT

When there are only two alternatives and both of them are known, an hypothesis contrary to fact may be true. "If the dog had not run into the road at this point, I would not have hit it," is quite true, if we know that the dog has bounded out of a completely safe place where the car could not have hit it. But to say, "If I had only not taken that road, I would not have hit a dog" is to disallow the quite possible mishap of hitting several playful dogs on an alternate route.

The wife who chides, "If you had only gone to church instead of the golf course you would not have had a heart attack," may be right. But how can she know? It is quite possible that lusty singing or a reaction touched off by the sermon of the morning might have precipitated an even worse heart attack.

The hypothesis contrary to fact takes on serious proportions in discussions of history and politics. "If St. Paul had not received his Macedonian call in a dream he would have gone east. Thus Asia would have been Christianized, and now we would be communists being cultivated by eastern Christian capitalists." "If Truman had not fired MacArthur we would never had had this Vietnam mess!" "If only the national election had gone the other way we would not be in another inflationary spiral." None of these "ifs," or others like them, and the consequences supposed to flow from them have any respectable standing in logical reasoning. Nor do any of the following.

A marine biologist recently conjectured, "If the horseshoe crab had reacted to competition in its environment and had thus specialized and diversified it would not have survived as long as it has." An advertisement confidently claims, "If Einstein were only alive today he would use Master-X computers and not a friend to check his mathematical calculations." An intoxicated girl in her jail cell moans, "If I had only gone to the Blue Note instead of this rock concert I wouldn't be having to call my father asking him to call his lawyer."

### 4. Begging the Question, or Petitio Principii

Begging the question is to some an unusual term for circular argumentation. More often than not begging the question involves statements rather than questions.

A physics professor was chiding a class for failing so

many pop quizzes. A brash freshman volunteered, "You are not handling the course right. If you would teach us the material then we would know it for the tests." The glowering professor withered the student with the retort, "You, Mr. Blithers, are begging the question!" The perplexed student protested later to an upperclassman, "There was no question in what I said. What did he mean—begging the question?" The upperclassman then defined the term for him. "One of the meanings of 'beg' is to assume without proof," he said. "To beg a question is to make one statement and then give support to it by repeating its essential meaning in slightly different words. And that's precisely what you did. Of course if he taught us the material then we would know it. But he wants us to learn to get it on our own."

Begging the question is sometimes less a fallacy, strictly speaking, than it is a useless exercise. Such is the fruitlessness of the apparent reasoning, "Risking one's life to save a drowning person is a selfish act for it is carried out by a self." Obviously. But one follows this with, "After all whatever a person does is done by himself and for himself. If he did not want to do it he would not have. But wanting to do it was selfish." This line of thinking ignores the fact that one might very much prefer not to take the risk. So two very different kinds of use of the term "selfish" are involved. Equivocation is blended here with circular reasoning, or begging the question.

Devout persons sometimes base their religious tenets upon these assertions: "I believe the Bible to be the Word of God. Why? Because the Bible itself says that it is inspired of God." If one literally means that he holds the belief for the reason he gives he is engaging in circular reasoning by letting a claim of a book confirm its own authority.

From a bountiful supply of instances of *petitio principii* the following are offered as representative of the fallacy. "If he would only slow down in his lectures I would be able to understand the material. Why can't I understand it now? He just goes too blamed fast." Child to parent: "If you would only give us as much allowance as we ask for, we wouldn't have to ask you for more money." To an English test question, "Why is plot considered first over character in a story?" a student responded, "Plot is always considered first over character in a story because character is considered second to plot." A village moralist advises, "Be what you is because if you be what you ain't then you ain't what you is!"

Occasionally an instance of begging the question proceeds by a somewhat eccentric circle, as in the following instance. A representative of a farmers' organization was discussing the difficulties involved in marketing farm products at a reasonable profit. "Consumers should realize," he said, "that ninety-five percent of what is good for the farmers is good for the urban consumer. And vice versa. Ninety-five percent of what is good for the urban consumer is good for the farmer." We are inclined to wonder about the other five percent of what is good for either or each. This is a variation on the historic observation of Charles E. Wilson about the mutual welfare of General Motors and the country.

Remember that begging the question is not to be confused with the putting of a leading question. The difference has already been noted in Chapter 1.

### 5. WELL POISONING

A rather effective device children use to protect a candy bar from an envious friend is to lick the bar all over and then ask, "Do you wanna bite?" Well poisoning is somewhat like this, for a speaker may wish to protect his position by enveloping it with something rather unpalatable.

A teacher may be tempted to limit the number of conferences which disrupt a comfortable schedule by saying to his class, "The points we have been discussing involve rather knotty problems, true. But the diligent, alert student should have derived from our analysis a clear understanding of them. My office hours are posted and I will discuss these points individually with any of you who do not understand them." Who is going to give evidence he is not diligent or alert by calling upon the professor for a conference?

A town councilman deliberately proposed well poisoning when he said, "Our strategy when we have the public meeting this evening with the zoning advocates will be to picture members of that group as being somehow in cahoots with those who want to build the shopping mall and stand to benefit by rezoning. Once that idea's planted with the audience they had better watch out."

Poisoning the well is frequently encountered in political situations where a speaker details at some length how "Anyone who opposes the military budget which has been proposed is bound to be uninformed about the needs for such a budget, or else willing to weaken our nation's hand in negotiation with potential enemies." Anyone who speaks in response to this is going to have to combine some personal courage with aptness in articulating his reasons in a way to neutralize the well poisoning.

Well poisoning is sometimes scarcely discernible from the *ad hominem* argument. If the speaker just mentioned has an opponent on the platform and pictures him as "a fuzzy minded, liberal idealist, a pacifist even, who just does not find himself able to come to grips with the reality of our situation in world affairs," he has poisoned the well.

What was wrong with the reasoning of the columnist, the psychic healer, and the commentator on our historic part in wars at the beginning of this chapter? The columnist was guilty of the misuse of analogy. The interplay of government and business is quite unlike the functioning of sports personnel in handling game situations, and also quite unlike court situations.

The psychic healer is engaging in circular reasoning and the man who would prefer that historic events had happened differently has developed some hypotheses contrary to fact.

### Exercises: Chapter 5

Label the following according to the fallacy each most aptly illustrates.

1. "Anybody knows what a vice is. It is anything that is not a virtue, just as a virtue is anything that is not a vice."

2. "That blocked kick just before the half! That's what lost us the game!"

3. A trustee responded to a reporter's question, "We were told this was to be an executive session and that we were not to breathe a word that was said."

4. "Assassins' bullets have changed history mightily. The Kennedy brothers and King together could have guaranteed us tranquility at home and friendly relations abroad and economic stability at the same time."

5. Herbert Spencer said that the state is like an individual organism: telegraph wires and railways are like the nerves and arteries of the organism and the organs of the governmental system are like the alimentary system in the organism.

6. "Campus and community violence in the 1960s produced corruption in the 1970s. As the president has

pointed out, 'If we had not had demonstrations, burn-
ings, crime, and disdain for law and order, Watergate
would not have happened. Disrespect for the law is
contagious.' "

7. "There are two sides to every question."

8. The mayor of a large industrial city said during a
strike, "What keeps people apart is the inability to
get together."

9. Advertisement: "We have made the impossible auto-
matic thermostat."

10. Sales manager to sales force: "I will be in my office
additional hours this week to help any who have been
goofing off, or who feel they haven't quite the ability
to keep pace in the current competitive market. Now,
a show of hands of those who wish conferences."

11. "Business is business," I always say.

12. "Educated people take no stock in any traditional
religious concepts."
"But I know some college graduates, even some Ph.
D.'s, who do."
"I said educated. They are not really educated or they
wouldn't."

13. Voter: "I agree with Senator Soundoff because his
position on issues is just like mine."

14. A man was arguing for the passage of a law requiring
news reporters to reveal their sources. He said, "For
a reporter to say, 'My source is confidential,' is just
like saying, 'My information came to me in a dream.' "

15. An appeal for subscribers for a newspaper reads, "This
paper is seventy-six years old, and yet as new as tomorrow."

16. A logic instructor ventured the notion that language
is related to thought as money is to business. Words,
he said, symbolize objects or ideas while money symbolizes goods or services.

17. "My economics professor knows what he is talking about when he says Keynesian economics is ruining the country. Anyone who sees so clearly what Keynesianism has done in the past few years has a keen insight into our country's situation."

18. "I am glad that my opponent for office is on the platform tonight for I can charge him openly with being favorable to oil interests. It follows, since he cannot deny such favoritism, that you must interpret anything he says in the light of that fact."

19. "How do you know *First Fling* is a rotten movie if you have not seen it?"
    "How do you know an egg is rotten if you have not eaten it?"

20. "Do you think," Voltaire has Candide ask, "That men have always massacred each other, as they do today, that they have been false . . . thieving, weak . . . greedy, drunken . . . hypocritical and stupid?"
    "Do you think," Voltaire has Martin rejoining, "that hawks have always eaten pigeons when they could find them?"
    "Of course," replied Candide.
    "Then," contended Martin, "if hawks have always had the same character, why should we suppose that men would change theirs?"

21. Following his often cited "A foolish consistency is the hobgoblin of little minds," Emerson went on to say, "With consistency a great soul has simply nothing to do. He may as well concern himself with his shadow on the wall."

22. "Every why hath a wherefore." Shakespeare, *Comedy of Errors,* act 2, scene 2.

23. "The *only safety* for the conquered is to expect no safety." Vergil, *Aeneid,* II, 354 .

24. Ovid, in *Metamorphoses,* endorses long hair on men

in lines like the following: "Don't tell me man-grown hair is out of fashion. A tree's not beautiful when grey and bare, a horse without his mane's not fit to look at. . . . So a deep-matted run of hair looks handsome on any man who has the luck to wear it."

25. Logic is very much like marriage. Each must be experienced to be truly appreciated. Both arouse much tension among those involved, but few who have tried them do not recommend a go at them.

### COMMENTS ON EXERCISES FOR CHAPTER 5

1. Begging the question. Or at any rate a circular negative attempt at definition.

2. Hypothesis contrary to fact. If the complaint is reworded this will be clear. "If that pre-half kick had not been blocked we would have won the game." Why do athletes sometimes berate themselves so about one bad play? The winning or losing of a game depends on a combination of numerous plays.

3. An internal inconsistency. Breathing the word that the trustees were not to breathe a word set off a great deal of speculation as to the darkness of the transactions handled in the meeting.

4. Hypothesis contrary to fact. With the three dead there is no way to assure what they might have accomplished.

5. Even great minds occasionally fall into error. In this case Spencer engages in misuse of analogy. There is a vast difference between a governmental system and an individual human being.

6. Hypothesis contrary to fact.

7. This assertion is internally inconsistent. Can there be two sides to the question as to whether or not there are

two sides to every question? If so, the assertion falls. If not, the assertion is false.

8. Begging the question, a circular statement.
9. Internal inconsistency.
10. Well poisoning. What salesman cares to imply goofing off or lack of competitive ability?
11. Taken literally, begging the question. In its customary use, this is an instance of equivocation. The speaker usually means, "Sharp dealing is all right in the realm of business affairs."
12. Begging the question.
13. Begging the question.
14. Misuse of analogy.
15. Internal inconsistency. How can anything be as "new as tomorrow"?
16. Misuse of analogy.
17. Begging the question.
18. Well poisoning.
19. A well-worn instance of misuse of analogy.
20. Misuse of analogy. There are quite some differences between hawks and human beings and one of these is that man has a much wider range of choices as to modes of actions than do hawks.
21. Misuse of analogy.
22. Begging the question.
23. Internal inconsistency.
24. Misuse of analogy.
25. Misuse of analogy.

# Chapter 6

# Subjectively Appealing Side Issues

Man's capabilities in communication are both marvelous and treacherous. So it is also with his capacity for emotional responses. He is driven through emotions to strive for legitimate self-concerns. He is motivated on behalf of others by his capacity to imagine what they are experiencing in their minds and feelings. And emotions and language are inextricably intertwined. Emotions can color our language and language can stir or calm our emotions. When either emotions or language lack control or direction trouble can result.

To the extent that emotions intrude upon our attempts to think through problems coolly to that extent we veer away from soundness in our reasoning. For example, a dialogue we sometimes encounter goes like this. "Those picketers are shiftless, no-good troublemakers who are hell bent on tearing down our institutions. And once they've torn them down they'll name one of their rotten bunch as a Fascist dictator who'll really enslave us." "Oh no. You've got them all wrong. They are an alert, perceptive group of concerned citizens whose clear-eyed perception of the deep meaning of our marvellous constitution has led them to assert their rights, and this will preserve sacred rights for all of us."

A candidate for national office traveled from place to place stressing state ownership of tideland oil and mineral rights in coastal states and national responsibility for aiding in developing all natural resources in inland states. He advocated preservation of wilderness areas where the Sierra Club was strong and criticized the government for too strict regulation of timberland and grazing lands where the Sierra Club was out of earshot.

"Sure I'm gonna vote for Congressman Svenson. He's a down-to-earth, plain sort of fellow. He campaigns a lot on foot and hardly ever fools with this expensive jet travel. Every chance he gets, whenever he can find a day or so off, he works at some common labor. That shows his working man's background. He talks plain, too. None of this highflown oratory for him."

The following discussion analyzes typical ways in which such intrusions as these appear.

## 1. EMOTIONAL LANGUAGE

Words, especially with the emphasis we may put upon them, often express emotion and arouse emotion in others. This is a good thing, for there are evils we should condemn and motivate others to avoid, and there are good deeds we wish to espouse in language to inspire their doing.

But the use of emotional language is not appropriate in discourse which is purportedly objective and analytic. Specialized forms of the use of emotional language have already been discussed: euphemisms, obscuration, humor, clichés, and well-poisoning. This section will be devoted to other forms of emotional language improperly used.

Expletives or profanity may express one's emotions and stir emotions in others, emotions which get in the way of constructive thinking. When one reacts to an editorial by muttering an eight-letter word for male bovine feces (pardon the euphemism), he is merely expressing a strong, averse, personal reaction. The objection to such an expletive is not so much that it is unesthetic as that it reflects a disinclination for reasoned rejoinder.

Two men were discussing drugs and the contemporary scene. The exponent of mind-expanding drugs described one who experienced "return trips" as a visionary mystic. "Visionary mystic" is more emotional as a phrase than logically precise. But the phrase is still not nearly as emotional as the words used by the debater who opposed the use of drugs. "Bull - - - -! You know goddamned well he's no visionary mystic. He's a cerebral paralytic whose feeble brain has been shot to hell." In such frantic debating it is difficult to get a meeting of minds on precise meanings of words and therefore a clear judgment on major issues.

Thomas Paine's *Common Sense* contained a good deal of emotional language which one would consider properly directed if one held that his thesis was ethically acceptable. But many of Paine's expressions were so emotional in tone that they hardly qualify as strictly logical propositions. For example, "Those who espouse the doctrine of reconciliation are . . . interested men who are not to be trusted, weak men who cannot see, prejudiced men who will not see and certain . . . immoderate men who think better of the . . . European world than it deserves. . . ."

The choice of words to color statements produced a game attributed to Bertrand Russell, the "conjugation of irregular words": "I am firm. You are obstinate. He is a pig-headed fool." "I am apt in assimilating material. You quote mighty freely. He is a shameless literary thief."

Some emotional language has its day and fades. "Nigger," "Red," "Commie" and similar labels now sometimes result in the user's finding himself the target of criticism. During one of many congressional investigations a prominent lawyer in a fit of pique spoke of a senator of Oriental descent as a "little Jap." Critical reaction was immediate and widespread, prompting an apology. The lawyer's initial response to the outcry was to protest feebly that he would not be offended at being called "an American" or "a Yank." But this was a poor analogy, for "American" is certainly a complimentary and not an offensive label, while "Jap" is. And "Yank" and "little Jap" fall in entirely different emotional categories.

The American Civil Liberties Union, despite its commendation by a politically balanced group of large and respected newspapers, receives highly emotional letters from various segments of the nation's citizenry. The letters condemn the organization, without offering any analysis of the policies of the Union. They use expressions like: "You are just a bunch of Communist hippies." "You filthy, mangy, fleabitten dogs." "You're the very devil in legal disguise."

Jews have to bear such taunts as, "I don't see why we should risk world war just because of a bunch of grasping, sharp-dealing Hebes who've got most of the moneyed power in this coutry." This was a response someone made regarding the question of aid for Israel.

Educators and educational administrators we can list this time as not the perpetrators but the targets of emotional language from both liberals and conservatives. A self-styled liberal student newspaper editorialized: "Our administrators, from student personnel directors on up, are just a bunch of old fogies whose stale notions come from the mid-Victorian, boring society of a generation ago." A conservative editorialist holds that the nation faces ruin because a "spineless, permissive educational practice sponsored by soft, addlepated, pseudo-educational technicians are producing gutless, gritless good-for-nothings."

Cautions about the misuse of emotional language are by no means new. Dr. Samuel Johnson was similar to contemporary analytic philosophers in his concern about emotional words. However, he seemed to think that we could be improved ethically by the elimination of pejorative or disparaging words from our vocabulary. Yet his famed dictionary contained emotionally charged wording in many definitions. He defined excise tax thus. "A hateful tax levied upon commodities, and adjudged not by the common judges of property, but wretches hired by those to whom the excise is paid." A stockjobber was, to Dr. Johnson, "A low wretch who gets money by buying and selling shares in funds." While a student at Pembroke, Samuel Johnson was penalized for missing a lecture and complained to the headmaster, "You have sconced me twopence for a lecture not worth a penny." But somewhere along the line, he decided that "sconce" was a word that should not be retained in usage. A good many words are still in use which Dr. Johnson thought should be eliminated, among them: dumbfound, gambler, ignoramus, simpleton and touchy!

## 2. APPEAL TO MISERY, OR ARGUMENTUM AD MISERICORDIAM

An appeal to misery or sympathy or pity is, like emotional language, not without ethical justification in

certain situations. A veteran who bears the crippling effects of war may deserve sympathy which may move others
to provide for his care generously from public funds, by
job training or through other measures. But to elect him to
a public office for which someone else is better qualified
is another matter.

No less a man than the "Father of Western Philosophy,"
Socrates, resorted to the appeal to pity in his trial before
the Athenian court. He reminded the court of earlier de-
fendants who had entreated them tearfully and brought
their children into court to play upon the court's sympathy.
And then, while declaring he would not resort to such
tactics, described himself to them as a man of flesh and
blood and the father of not yet grown sons!

Sometimes, at least ethically or humanely speaking, one
must make decisions as to whether or not an appeal to
misery is having undue weight. A juror may vote to acquit
a man simply because conviction and penalty, though
clearly merited by the facts in the case, would prove embar-
rassing to the man and his family. This would be succumb-
ing to an appeal to misery. However, if the crime is not
enormous and the penalty would deprive a family of necessary support, a vote to acquit might be in order. However,
sanely and logically written laws would provide for alternative penalties, probation, or other means of handling
the situation justly.

Certainly it is a question of serious import as to whether
an incompetent in a position of responsibility should be
continued in his post simply because he had an unhappy
childhood, or whether a vote should be swayed toward a
mediocre candidate for office because he is dependent
upon veterans' disability benefits for his support.

The appeals made by charitable groups deserve discussion. For example, those concerned with fighting heart disease, curing arthritis, and eliminating child abuse, to list only a few. Sympathy can get out of hand so that donations jeopardize a personal budget that otherwise might enable one to contribute more effectively toward wider solutions to social problems. Emotional appeals may attract support of less important groups at cost of others.

### 3. APPEAL TO SPECIAL TASTES

Special pleading is a fallacy in which one takes up his own cause in his own interests. Appeal to special tastes occurs when someone discerns what an individual's special interest is or what a group's special interests are and caters to them.

Marketing research was well underway when the twentieth century dawned. What the marketing researcher did was to contract with a manufacturer, say, to direct his advertising at those likely to purchase the product rather than depend upon a more random spray of advertisements. This serves the public and the producer well, as long as it remains within the confines of meeting needs.

More recently, however, interests and tastes have been the target of advertisers who play upon one's latent desires in order to make a sale. The question "What kind of man reads *Playboy?*" with its accompanying photographs, attracts men of a certain age and income bracket to subscribe to the magazine. Subtly, such an advertisement also appeals to men in a lower income or higher age bracket who wish they were that kind of man.

Religious books and periodicals direct their sales pitch to ministers, church school teachers and active church members. These persons may already have been saturated with religious materials and should look to a broadening of their interests. But because of appeals to their special tastes they continue to expand their libraries with literature of a limited kind.

"Go Where the Boys Are!" is the caption of a beach resort advertisement in a journal directed at young women. "The Great Getaway Machine" is an appeal to those who like motorcycling and nature. "Our backpacking equipment is tough as an armadillo shell" claims an advertisement in a natural history publication. "You can get a Simple Interest Loan for practically anything" promises a notice in a state employees' journal. And from a politician comes somewhat different appeals: at a naturalists' rally, "Our pledge is to expand wildlife preserves"; and later to a chamber of commerce, "Ecologists are playing on our emotions. We can build more industry here and I will work to that end."

Advertisers of tobacco products use the pages (one is tempted to use the emotional phrase "pollute the pages") of publications with their appeals to special tastes. A cigarette advertisement declares that a particular cigarette is not for everybody, implying that only the tobacco connoisseur appreciates it. This could be construed, of course, as an appeal to popular rather than special taste because of the rather general desire of individuals to be in a special class. Another capitalizes on the women's liberation movement by numerous advertisements about what a long way, you, baby, have come. In a more male chauvinist vein is the cigarette advertisement picturing a beautiful model, cigarette in hand, with the caption, "For More of a Woman —and for More of a Cigarette."

Occasionally, but all too rarely, a political figure dares to be logical and consistent, refusing to appeal to special tastes and venturing even possibly to offend those who have

special interests. This was the case when President Gerald
Ford appeared before a veterans' convention and issued an
appeal for leniency toward Vietnam service evaders.

### 4. APPEAL TO POPULAR TASTES OR ARGUMENTUM AD POPULUM

In defining the appeal to popular tastes we encounter
something on the order of an argument of the beard. What
is the dividing line between appealing to special and appealing to popular tastes? A traditional illustration of the
appeal to popular tastes, or the *argumentum ad populum,*
is the revered trio "flag, motherhood, and apple pie."
These do have wide appeal, but a pettifogger might note
that zero population growth has modified regard for
motherhood and that apple pie does not dominate the
dessert scene. But the point is that an appeal such as this
reaches at least a segment of each of the various special
groups we encounter. Ecologists as well as industrialists,
old as well as young, male as well as female furnish large
numbers who salute the flag, respect their mothers, and
frequently eat apple pie.

The fallacy should interest us when such appeals become
irrelevant to something we are concerned about. When a
politician stages a cookout and presides over the barbecue
pit, does that mean he can handle the intricate tasks required of a legislator? When a minister shows himself an
authority on baseball, does that qualify him for theological
and ethical judgments? When a professor plays a mean
game of bridge, does that indicate he is a good physiologist?

A bumper sticker slogan reads "If you outlaw guns, only
outlaws will have guns." This appeal to popular tastes is
absurd because no one has proposed relieving law officers
of their weapons. An automobile commercial associates a
particular brand of car with love for baseball, hot dogs, and

apple pie. A cereal manufacturer packages the cereal in a carton picturing harvesting of grain by hand with lettering of an earlier period urging, "Get back to nature and to the basic things of life. Eat Frontierland Hearty Cereal." Even if wheat were harvested today by hand, what difference would it make in the quality of food value of the cereal?

When tobacco products are promoted by pictures of frontier life, when a whiskey is associated with men in overalls leisurely making charcoal for the processing of the whiskey, or when a breakfast food has grandpa playing with the children, an appeal is being made to popular and quite likely irrelevant tastes.

A young college instructor was clearly a victim of entrapment since he had tried to resist an appeal from a new but very persistent friend to secure some marijuana for him just to experiment with one time, and had also tried to decline any money for the marijuana. But the prosecuting attorney secured a conviction and a very heavy penalty through contrasting his general activities with that of two retired professors who had taught Sunday school classes for years, enjoyed gardening, had fine families (the defendant was single), and were giants in the field of education. This was very clearly an appeal based upon popular tastes and interest.

The two estimates of the picketers reported at the first of this chapter were clearly thrown out of balance by the emotional coloring of those estimates. The traveling candidate was guilty of appealing to special tastes or interests in the various states he visited. And Congressman Svenson is gaining support by traits that appeal to popular tastes.

### Exercises: Chapter 6

Label the following according to the fallacy each most aptly illustrates.

1. "She is the only child, the darling of her parents. To suspend her from school would be to break their hearts. I vote she be allowed to continue."

2. "No wonder crime is rampant. Officers are handicapped by having to get warrants, having to inform a suspect of his rights and all that tripe. I say that you and I as common people, down to earth, straightforward, honest people should band together to see that the guilty are apprehended and punished promptly with no nonsense!"

3. An advertisement for a hotel on a Mediterranean strand reads: "What's so great about a white Christmas? B-r-r-r-r! Spend your midwinter vacation swimming and golfing in the Mediterranean sun!"

4. A veteran was attempting to sell several magazine subscriptions to a lady who had just invested all she could afford in periodicals being sold by a local school group. He complained bitterly, "So you'd turn down a veteran who was wounded in the service of his country so a bunch of young'uns can get a trip to Washington? You got no feeling at all about a man who's down and out."

5. "That eyebrow twitching, stuttering, bloated, Bible-spouting senator ought to quit his witchhunting and get back to the business of serving the people of his state."

6. Student charged before the student council with a rather serious breach of regulations regarding alcohol: "Please let me off, or at least give me some punishment that won't appear on the record. My father is chairman of the temperance committee in our church and he'd feel disgraced by this."

7. "Vote for Walldraggle for senator. He's the people's choice."

8. "Gee whiz! I've only got a 1.72 quality point ratio, sir. I've gotta have a B on this course!" (A 2.0 quality point ratio is required for the student to remain in college.)

9. Churchmember: "Let's try to get that preacher. He's just like us. He likes grits and red-eye gravy, works a garden in overalls, hunts and fishes, thinks golf is ritzy and sissy, and talks from the pulpit like he does on the street."

10. Girl who has just missed an announced test: "But, sir, my boyfriend just left for his physical under the draft. I was just too blue to take the test."

11. Thrasymachus, according to Plato's Republic, vexed by Socrates' continual questioning, charged Socrates with having a poor nurse who let him snivel, never wiped his nose and did not teach him the difference between a shepherd and his sheep.

12. "Yes, he failed three courses and had only Ds in others, placing him below our standards for retention. But, after all, he is a good citizen and his father is one of our wealthier trustees. Let's let him continue."

13. Advertisement showing a slender, charming girl attracting the attention of a male viewer: "For that indelible impression use Dietabs."

14. Marc Antony's funeral oration declared that Caesar wept when the poor cried, was modest and not ambitious, turned down a proffered king's crown three times. He declared too that he himself was just a plain, blunt man who loved the Caesar who was so generous to his subjects.

15. Letter to editor: "This publisher's open letter to the senator was completely fair-minded and unassailable in its logic. It remains to be seen, then, whether the senator will listen to the calm voice of reason or

whether his head will be further turned by the ridiculous adulation recently showered upon him at a rally."

16. An enterprising salesman in the 1972 campaign period is reported to have worn a Nixon button when calling on Republican prospects and a "Vote Democratic" button when calling on Democrats.

17. Presiding officer at a political rally: "A vote cast for this great leader is a vote for all the things that America stands for! It is a vote for the flag! It is a vote for the sanctity of the family! It is a vote for restoring religion to our godless schools! And it is a vote for the working man!"

18. During the 1976 bicentennial observation, a travel folder and guide described a certain historic spot in this fashion: "It was here that the Father of our country met with his brilliant, faithful and intrepid counselors for a crucial strategy session. Later it fell, but only temporarily, into the hands of greedy henchmen of that idiotically unbalanced tyrant, the King of England."

19. Insurance salesman: "Sixteen of your fraternity brothers have the policy I'm offering you."

20. Clarence Darrow, eminent criminal lawyer of the early part of this century, pleading a case: "I appeal to you to free Thomas Kidd from the conspiracy charge. He comes from a long line of downtrodden people and was raised in poverty. His father and he were up before day to work in a coal mine and stopped after dark so they rarely saw the light of a sunny day. He never knew what a full, delicious meal was."

## COMMENTS ON EXERCISES FOR CHAPTER 6

1. Appeal to misery.
2. Primarily an appeal to popular tastes. As in most sub-

jective appeals there is a touch of emotional language.
3. Appeal to special tastes.
4. Appeal to misery, and use of emotional language.
5. Emotional language.
6. Appeal to misery.
7. Appeal to popular tastes. In this form this is what is sometimes called the "bandwagon appeal."
8. Appeal to misery.
9. Appeal to popular tastes.
10. Appeal to misery.
11. Emotional language.
12. Appeal to special tastes. The manner in which an appeal is made suggests that appeal to force may be implied.
13. Appeal to special tastes, or possibly appeal to popular tastes.
14. Appeal to popular tastes.
15. Emotional language.
16. The salesman may have been enterprising but he was less than frank and open about his political commitments as he engaged in appealing to special tastes or interests very likely in a manner in no way related to his product.
17. Such phraseology as this is traditionally presented as an appeal to popular tastes. Some might argue that those to whom such an appeal would be effective have shrunken in number so that this would have to be listed as an appeal to special tastes.
18. Emotional language first of a favorable kind and then of a quite unfavorable kind.
19. An appeal to special tastes.
20. Darrow frequently used such an appeal to misery.

# Part 2

# Rules Governing Inference

Two words that are often misused in commonplace discourse are the words "imply" and "infer." A simple rule governing the general use of these two words is this: A speaker or writer may make a statement that *implies,* or conveys meaning (sometimes more meaning than is actually stated) by the words used, while a hearer or reader *infers* meaning (again, sometimes more meaning than the words actually state) from the words uttered or written.

For example, if one says, "Israel and Egypt are at war again," since war *implies* violence, he is saying that violence has broken out, though not in just these words. The hearer *infers* from the disconcerting announcement, "Violence has been resorted to between Israel and Egypt." The words are improperly used in two ways. First, they are sometimes interchanged so that a speaker or writer is said to "infer by his statement" or, more rarely, a hearer

or reader is said to "imply from a statement." The customary usage goes thus: a speaker or writer implies while a
hearer or reader infers.

Second, we sometimes imply by careless choice of words
or by inflection more than we intend to or should, and
sometimes we infer from statements more than we should.
In the portion of the study we have just concluded we
have encountered a lot of implying and a lot of inferring,
largely in the psychological sense. That is the case in instances where, let us say, an advertisement implies something but in a subtle, often misleading way and the viewer
of the advertisement infers something not strictly justified.
An advertisement may imply or hint at the notion that
your itchy skin may be psoriasis. If you hurry out to buy a
bottle of Exo-Psoriasis without consulting a dermatologist
you have improperly inferred just what the cosmetic
company probably wanted you to infer.

The earlier part of this study was intended to caution
against careless psychological inference. An appeal was
implied, in the commonplace sense of the term implied,
throughout that one should exercise care and infer, in the
commonplace sense of the term infer, no more than the
words actually convey, and sometimes not to infer anything
at all from some assertions.

We now turn to a study of implying (implication) and
inferring (inference) in a much more precise, detailed and
extended fashion. That is, we shall be using the terms in
the more strict, logical sense in which logicians use the
terms.

By *inference* logicians usually mean the mental process
in which a person passes from one assertion or several
assertions to another assertion, a conclusion. There are
*emotional* or *psychological* inferences, and the informal
fallacies arise from these. There are also formal or logical

inferences. These must abide by the rules of logic and not be determined by one's own emotional or psychological bias.

By *implication* logicians usually mean the logical relationship between propositions such that one proposition is asserted to follow necessarily from another proposition or set of propositions. A relationship of implication is an objective fact in the sense that it is independent of one's wishes or emotional processes.

Let us examine the following illustration. According to a principle of arithmetic called commutation, the acceptance of the fact that $1 + 2 = 3$ implies necessarily that $2 + 1 = 3$. This relationship of implication between $1 + 2 = 3$ and $2 + 1 = 3$ is a fact, whether anyone infers it or not. Thus, I can infer logically, that is, I can engage in a process of reasoning, that $2 + 1 = 3$ necessarily derives from $1 + 2 = 3$.

A great part of this section will deal with what is called *mediate inference*. Mediate inference is the process of deriving a conclusion from two propositions called premises. The premises have a middle or mediating term which links two other terms. One of the premises also serves as a link between the other premise and the conclusion. Here is an illustration.

> All spiders are eight-legged creatures.
> All tarantulas are spiders.
> Therefore all tarantulas are eight-legged creatures.

"Spider" serves to mediate between or link the terms "tarantulas" and "eight-legged creatures." "All tarantulas are spiders" also links the other premise with the conclusion.

One chapter will be devoted to *immediate* or *direct* *inference*. Immediate inference goes like this. Given a single proposition, several other propositions may be drawn from it without the aid of a mediating term or proposition. Here is an illustration.

Let us suppose that it is true that "All politicians are extroverts." We may conclude without the aid of a second premise that the following are also true:

> Some politicians are extroverts.
> No politicians are introverts.
> Some politicians are not introverts.

Normally in the portion of the work that is to follow, we shall demand that a proposition be stated so that what it implies or involves is clear. We will depart from this principle only occasionally and then to use meaningless symbols or nonsense terms in order to show that patterns of logic are independent of material truth or intelligible content. We shall insist that the subject and predicate of a proposition be explicit as to their relationship. Is all of the subject to be included in the predicate or excluded from the predicate? Is part of the subject to be included in the predicate or excluded from the predicate?

We shall also insist when two propositions are stated with the purpose of deriving a third proposition from them that they follow strict rules that will make the conclusion necessarily, not merely probably or possibly, follow.

Mediate inference, which will be dealt with first, involves several syllogistic forms. A syllogism is a process of reasoning involving two propositions and a conclusion drawn from the relationship of the two propositions. The "syl" part of the word has evolved from the Greek word *syn,* meaning with. The "logism" part derives from the Greek word *logos,* from which we get both "-logy" meaning study of, and "logic" meaning reasoning. Thus, when two propositions are placed with each other in a relationship for which it is claimed that additional information—a conclusion—is forced upon us, we have a syllogism. The syllogism may or may not be valid, depending upon a variety of factors.

There are various kinds of syllogisms. One is the *categorical syllogism,* the subject of the first chapter in this section. Others are the *hypothetical syllogism,* the *alternative syllogism,* the *disjunctive syllogism,* and the *combination of the alternative and disjunctive syllogisms.*

A categorical statement is a direct assertion, simple and straightforward with no "if," "and," or "but" qualifying it. A categorical syllogism is constructed of three such propositions, two serving as premises and the third as a conclusion.

Hypothetical statements express or imply an "if." Thus the hypothetical syllogism consists of a major premise conditionally stated with an "if," a minor premise categorically stated, and a conclusion also categorically stated.

The other types of statements and the syllogisms based upon them will be left for definition later on. We now turn to the categorical syllogism. We will spend the most time on it, for it is basic to logical reasoning and other forms of the syllogism can often be rephrased in categorical form. Rephrasing syllogisms in other forms, for example hypothetical to categorical or vice versa, often serves to double check one's analysis of the original syllogism.

# Chapter 7

# The Categorical Syllogism

"Sound businesses are those which showed a profit during that final, difficult quarter of last year. Able Associates made an excellent profit during that very period. So I'm investing in Able Associates stock."

"Those who are not engaged in marketing and management will not need to subscribe to our magazine, *Profits and Losses*. But you are engaged in marketing and management. Therefore you should subscribe immediately."

"Receiving federal grants means that our university will be subject to governmental interference in the management of our affairs. We are declining to accept any such grant so that we will be free of any governmental regulations."

Neither of these commonly advanced arguments is valid. The fallacies that are involved and other fallacies related to them following categorical syllogistic processes now engage our attention.

## 1. THE STRUCTURE OF THE CATEGORICAL SYLLOGISM

The structure of the categorical syllogism is really very simple and it is in its simplicity primarily that its value and usefulness lie. The categorical syllogism consists of:
1. a proposition called a major premise
2. a second proposition called a minor premise
3. a third proposition called the conclusion

This type of syllogism also contains three and only three terms: a major term, a minor term and a middle term, the term that connects the major and minor terms. Here is an example with the terms identified by numbers:

$$\phantom{xxxxxxxxxxxx}1\phantom{xxxxxxxxxxxxxxx}2$$
Major Premise: All *good students* are *industrious*.
$$\phantom{xxxxxxxxxx}3\phantom{xxxxxxxxxxx}1$$
Minor Premise: *Meg* is a *good student*.
$$\phantom{xxxxx}3\phantom{xxxxxxx}2$$
Conclusion: *Meg* is *industrious*.

A little drill at this point will prove very helpful for what is to come. The predicate term of the conclusion is called the *major* term, and "P" is the standard symbol for the major term. The subject term of the conclusion is called the *minor* term, and "S" is the standard symbol for the minor term. The premises in which these terms appear are named accordingly the major premise and the minor premise.

The third term, which always appears once in each of the premises, is called the *middle* term, and "M" is the standard symbol for the middle term. Labeling the syllogism just used above, beginning with the conclusion, remember, results in the following:

$$\phantom{xxxxxxxxxxxx}M\phantom{xxxxxxxxxxxxxx}P$$
Major premise: All *good students* are *industrious*.
$$\phantom{xxxxxxxxxx}S\phantom{xxxxxxxxxxx}M$$
Minor Premise: *Meg* is a *good student*.

         S      P
Conclusion: *Meg* is *industrious.*

In the categorical syllogism qualifying words like "all" or "some," called *quantifiers,* must be made explicit. Later we shall drop the word "all" when we rewrite syllogisms in shortened, convenient form and place a small "d" beside the S, P or M to indicate that *all* is intended to apply to the term. The "d" is the initial letter of the word "distributed," a word used to denote that the entire membership of the class to which the term applies is included.

We shall also, to make work more efficient and accurate, omit the use of verbal connectives and use instead symbols meaning "included in" or "excluded from." A sidewise "V" pointing left will mean included in, and a sidewise "V" with a slash or vertical line through it will mean excluded from. (Students using Braille will find suggestions in the appendix of help in adapting symbols.) The syllogism used as an illustration above would appear in rewritten form thus:

       d M        P
    Good stud. $<$ ind.
       d S        M
    Meg $<$ good stud.
       d S     P
    Meg $<$ ind.

Note that Meg is quantified with a "d" because a single term or singular instance is *always* distributed. The nineteenth century English economist and logician, William S. Jevons, noted in his *Elementary Lessons in Logic,* "A singular proposition is a universal one; for it clearly refers to the whole subject, which in this case is a single individual thing."

The syllogism we have used as an illustration is valid in that it meets all of the conditions for a valid syllogism, the rules for which are the main topic of this chapter. For the moment we can demonstrate how the conclusion follows necessarily from the premises.

Let a large, open circle represent the major (P) term, "industrious persons." The circle is left open because the term is not distributed. That is, the class of industrious persons is indefinitely extended and we are not thinking in terms of *all* of the class.

Now let a second circle represent the middle (M) term, "good students," placing it within the large, open circle. Next place a third circle representing the minor (S) term, "Meg," within the second circle. If S (Meg) is inside M (good students) and if M (all good students) is inside P then S (Meg) must be inside P (industrious persons). The conclusion is forced upon us, and, thus, the syllogism is valid.

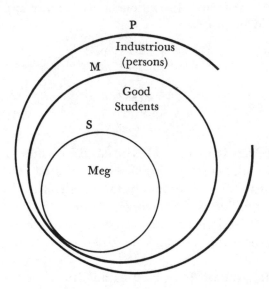

## 2. Notes on Some Important Terms

The syllogism above was said to be valid. *Validity,* *truth,* and *reliability* do not mean the same thing. Without involving complex philosophical arguments, let us agree that *truth* means that a statement conforms to what we accept as a fact. *Valid* in logical usage means that propositions are so related that a conclusion is forced upon us. If the conclusion is not forced by the logical relation of the terms in the syllogism, the syllogism must have some fallacy in it. *Reliable* applies only to the conclusion, and it means that the premises are accepted as true and their relationship has forced the acceptance of the conclusion. If the conclusion is indeed reliable, one has engaged in what some simply call sound thinking.

Suppose in the syllogism we have represented Meg as a good student when in fact she is not. The syllogism would be valid but the conclusion would not be reliable. One would suppose that the major premise, "All good students are industrious," is true by definition of what constitutes a good student. But if this is not accepted as the case the conclusion is even more unreliable.

## 3. Forms of Categorical Propositions

Categorical propositions are stated in four ways:
  A-form:  Universal Affirmative. "All good students are industrious."
  I-form:  Particular Affirmative. "Some good students overwork."
  E-form:  Universal Negative. "No good students are lazy."
  O-form:  Particular Negative. "Some good students do not overwork."
These designations derive from certain vowels in the two Latin words *AffIrmo,* I affirm; and *nEgO,* I deny. Some unknown and unsung logician hit upon the shorthand,

timesaving designations for the four kinds of propositions, A, I, E and O. The terms *AffIrmo* and *nEgO* also give us a helpful mnemonic device. Who can forget the designations after once observing the derivation?

### 4. THE DISTRIBUTION OF TERMS

a. *The A-Form Proposition: Universal Affirmative*

When a term of a proposition is intended to cover *all* instances of the membership of the class that term represents it is said to be "distributed." Let us use as an illustration the major premise in the syllogism analyzed a few paragraphs back, "All good students are industrious." In strict logical form this should be stated, "All good students are included in industrious persons." In the convenient shorthand of logic this proposition may be represented thus:

$$\overset{d}{\text{Good stud.}} < \text{ind.}$$

Note that neither term has been labeled S, P or M for when a proposition stands alone one cannot determine the major, minor or middle term. These labels are assigned in regard to the location of the terms in a syllogism. This is an A-form proposition, a universal affirmative. In it the subject, "good students," is distributed and the predicate, "industrious" ("persons" understood) is undistributed, for industrious persons extends indefinitely beyond good students.

Let a large, open circle represent "industrious persons," for we do not know or care for the moment how many "industrious persons" there are. Actually it is not a matter of our knowing how many there are. It is rather that in a proposition of the "All S is P" type "S" refers to all of the members of the class "S" while "P" does not refer to all of the members of the class "P". Now place a smaller closed circle within the large, open circle, the smaller circle representing "All good students," and the distribution of the one term and the lack of distribution of the other will be graphically clear.

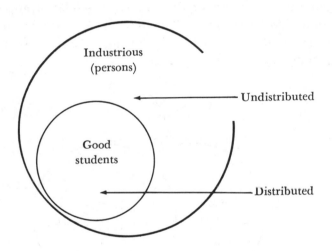

### b. *The I-Form Proposition: Particular Affirmative*

In the I-Form, or particular affirmative proposition, neither the subject nor the predicate is distributed for only *some* and not *all* is intended in each term. For example, "Some good students overwork," or in our shortened expression:

Good stud. < overwork.

Neither term is quantified by a "d" and so the statement can be read, "Some good students are included in the class of those persons who overwork." This time, two overlapping, open circles will represent the relationship of the undistributed terms. Where the circles overlap an area is mutually occupied and this may be represented by placing an "X" in the area.

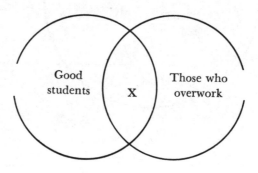

## c. *The E-Form Proposition: Universal Negative*

In the E-form, or universal negative proposition, both the subject and the predicate terms are distributed, for "All good students" are excluded from "*all* lazy persons," or

$$\overset{d}{\text{Good stud.}} \nless \overset{d}{\text{lazy.}}$$

This time we will use two closed circles representing all of each of the two classes and place them apart so that they do not overlap. This shows graphically that all good students stand completely apart from all lazy persons.

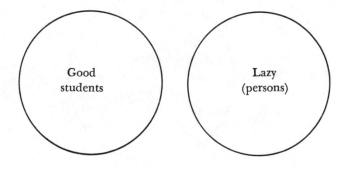

### d. *The O-Form Proposition: Particular Negative*

In the O-form, or particular negative proposition, the subject term is undistributed while the predicate term is distributed: "Some good students" are excluded from "all persons who overwork," or

$$\text{Good stud.} \overset{d}{\not\subset} \text{overwork.}$$

This time we shall let an open circle representing "Some good students" overlap a closed circle representing "All persons who overwork." The open circle is occupied, but we do not know to what extent. We place an "X" in a part of the good students' circle to indicate that a part of

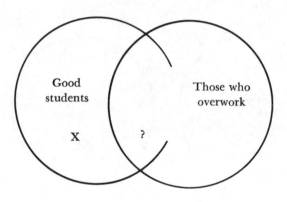

that circle is occupied. But notice that we are directed to place the "X" in that part of the circle which lies outside the circle of those who overwork. "Some good students are excluded from all those who overwork," this says. Some good students may lie inside the circle of those who overwork, but this we do not know from the original proposition.

Occasionally, a student has difficulty grasping the concept of distribution, and it might have been helpful if logicians had come up with a clearer term. If the matter proves puzzling despite our attempt to clarify the principle, one may just commit to memory the following pattern in which a "d" is placed over distributed terms and no designation over undistributed terms. Some authors place a "u" over undistributed terms but we will usually not use this notation.

$$
\begin{array}{lcc}
 & \overset{d}{} & \\
\text{A-form:} & \text{Subject} < \text{Predicate} \\
\text{I-form:} & \text{Subject} < \text{Predicate} \\
 & \overset{d}{} & \overset{d}{} \\
\text{E-form:} & \text{Subject} \not< \text{Predicate} \\
 & & \overset{d}{} \\
\text{O-form:} & \text{Subject} \not< \text{Predicate}
\end{array}
$$

Note the following pattern using both "d" and "u":

$$
\begin{array}{llll}
\text{A:} & d & < & u \\
\text{I:} & u & < & u \\
\text{E:} & d & \not< & d \\
\text{O:} & u & \not< & d
\end{array}
$$

We shall let the matter of distribution rest a bit and return to the significance of distribution in determining the validity of a syllogism later.

## 5. RULES GOVERNING THE CATEGORICAL SYLLOGISM

### a. *The Four-Term Fallacy*

*To be valid a syllogism must contain three and only three terms.* Constructing a syllogism with only two terms is usually quite awkward, and, when it occurs, is usually so clearly circular reasoning that this sort of fallacy does not merit attention.

If a line of reasoning presents more than three terms it is impossible to handle it in a single syllogism. Two or more syllogisms are required when more than three terms are being considered, depending upon how many terms are presented.

An obvious illustration of the four-term fallacy is the old play on words:

> Gold is heavy.
> Mary has a heart of gold.
> Therefore Mary's heart is heavy.

"Gold" is here used in two different senses and so is "heavy." "Gold in the first premise is the valuable metal with the chemical symbol Au, usually yellow, with an atomic weight of 197.2, etc. In the second premise, "gold" is used figuratively as descriptive of a generous disposition. We have two terms already. "Heavy" in the first premise, as it applies to gold, has to do with weight in the physical sense. "Heavy" in the conclusion is a figurative term for sad. We have four terms already. Actually there are five terms, for we must include "Mary's heart." At least it is used in the same sense both times it appears to refer to Mary's mood or disposition. A fallacy due to any number of terms other than three is usually called a "four-term fallacy."

In the following illustration the terms are numbered for easy identification of the four terms:

1                2

*Aiding both Arabs and Jews* is *a dangerous game.*

3                1

*Furnishing arms to both Arabs and Jews* is *aiding them.*

3

Therefore *furnishing arms to both Arabs and Jews will*

4

*cause Russia to take sides.*

Let us use three circles to show the difficulty we encounter in trying to represent these relationships graphically. Let a large, open circle represent term 2, "a dangerous game." Place within that circle another circle representing term 1, "Aiding both Arabs and Jews." Place within the inner circle a still smaller one representing term 3, "Furnishing arms to both Arabs and Jews."

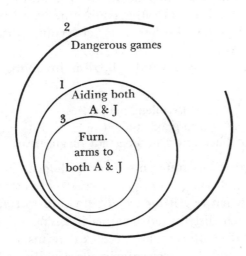

2 Dangerous games

1 Aiding both A & J

3 Furn. arms to both A & J

What forces us to conclude from the propositions anything at all about Russia's probable action? In logic we are interested solely in forced conclusions. We are not instructed where to place a circle representing Russia's taking sides with relation to the other circles.

The eighteenth century Swiss mathematician Leonhard Euler demonstrated the helpfulness and general adequacy of three circles to test the validity of an Aristotelian syllogism, such as those with which we are dealing. If we used a fourth circle to represent the term "cause Russia to take sides," we could not determine from the two premises where to place the circle. We cannot apply Euler's circles to either Mary's situation or the Arab-Israeli problem.

b. *The Fallacy of the Odd Negative,* or *Faulty Exclusions*

A valid syllogism must either have no negatives or exclusions, or it must have exactly two, one of which must be in the conclusion. The arrangement of negatives so that one is in a premise and one in the conclusion does not necessarily or automatically assure the validity of the syllogism, for some other rule governing distribution may be broken.

The following is a valid syllogism involving negative propositions.

> No good student plagiarizes.
> Don is a good student.
> Therefore Don does not plagiarize.

For practice let us state this in strict logical format, abbreviating and using appropriate labels. It is a very good procedure when rewriting a syllogism thus to first place a "d" over each distributed term as it is encountered and then label the subject and predicate terms of the conclusion "S" and "P" respectively and finally to label the terms of the premises "S," "P," and "M."

<table>
<tr><td></td><td>d M</td><td>d P</td></tr>
</table>

|                 | d M          |   | d P    |
|-----------------|--------------|---|--------|
| Major premise:  | Good stud. ⊀ plag. | | |
|                 | d S          |   | M      |
| Major premise:  | Don < good stud. | | |
|                 | d S          | d P |      |
| Conclusion:     | Don ⊀ plag.  |   |        |

This syllogism meets all of the requirements for valid syllogisms, both those discussed thus far and those to be discussed later, and therefore is valid.

Using circles to test the validity of the syllogism, let a large circle, closed to indicate the term is distributed, represent those who plagiarize. Place another closed circle representing good students outside the first circle. These circles represent clearly the mutual exclusion of good students and those who plagiarize. Then place a third circle representing Don inside the circle representing good students. Since Don is within the circle of good students which lies entirely outside the circle of those plagiarizing, then he, too, must lie outside the circle of plagiarists.

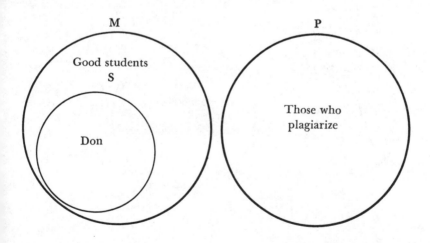

The following syllogism is invalid.

> Jehovah's Witnesses do not become five-star generals.
> Mervin is not a five-star general.
> Therefore Mervin is a Jehovah's Witness.

Or, in logical shorthand and format:

$$d \; P \qquad\qquad d \; M$$
$$\text{JWs} \; \nless \; \text{5-star gens.}$$
$$d \; S \qquad\qquad d \; M$$
$$\text{Merv} \; \nless \; \text{5-star gens.}$$
$$d \; S \qquad\qquad P$$
$$\text{Merv} \; < \; \text{JWs}$$

Again, using circles, let one closed circle represent Jehovahs' Witnesses and another closed circle represent five-star generals, the two being placed entirely apart. A circle representing Mervin must be placed outside the circle representing five-star generals, but this does not require placing the circle representing Mervin within the Jehovah's Witnesses' circle.

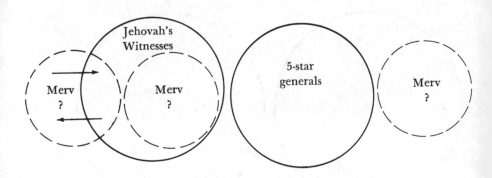

Mervin may lie outside both of the larger circles. He may indeed be a Jehovah's Witness and properly lie within that circle. But this we do not know. It is pressing the point a bit, but a circle representing Mervin could be placed overlapping the circle representing the Jehovah's Witnesses. This could illustrate that Mervin is either joining the Jehovah's Witnesses or is leaving that denomination.

Here is another example of an invalid syllogism.

> Some Christians are pacifists.
> No Christians are perfect.
> Therefore some who are perfect are pacifists.

Presented in logical format this would be:

$$\begin{array}{cc} M & P \\ \text{Xns.} < & \text{pac.} \\ d\ M & d\ S \\ \text{Xns.} \not< & \text{perf.} \\ S & P \\ \text{Perf.} < & \text{pac.} \end{array}$$

This syllogism breaks the rule that if one premise is negative, the conclusion must be negative. Testing with circles, let an open circle represent the undistributed term "pacifists." Place a closed circle representing the distributed term "Christians" overlapping the open circle. Place an "X" in the overlapping portion of the circles indicating that the space is occupied by at least some Christians. But now where would one place a closed circle representing the distributed term "perfect persons"? The circle has to be placed entirely apart from the circle representing "Christians." But where would it fall? It does not necessarily fall over the circle representing pacifists, but it could. We must always remember that we are interested only in forced conclusions, and in this case we are not directed by the premises to a specific placing of this circle.

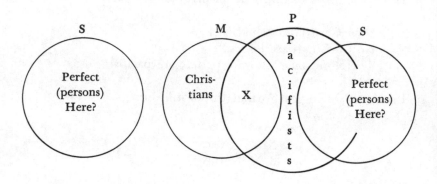

## c. *The Fallacy of the Undistributed Middle*

For a categorical syllogism to be valid the middle term must be distributed at least once in the premises. If the middle term is not distributed in one premise or the other the fallacy of the undistributed middle has been committed.

This fallacy is perhaps the one most frequently encountered in dealing with the categorical syllogism. The fallacy is somewhat similar to the fallacy of hasty generalization.

It is sometimes involved in the *ad hominem* fallacy and in instances of guilt by association.

Remember that some of the various kinds of fallacies discussed in earlier pages involve psychological quirks as well as, and sometimes rather than, logical fallacies as such. Some types of emotional imbalance produce the following kind of "reasoning."

d P         M
Napoleon was short of stature.
d S     M
I am short of stature.
d S     d P
Therefore I am Napoleon.

It would probably be futile to try to show our emotionally unbalanced friend that he is committing the fallacy of the undistributed middle. But that is what he is doing, even if it is his psychological mechanism that is leading him into error.

The following syllogism deals with an emotionally charged issue but it is one in which there is some hope of persuasive correction. Suppose someone says, "All feminists advocate abortion, and since Ms. Sterne advocates abortion she must surely be a feminist." Stating this argument in strict logical form, we have:

d P      M
Feminist < adv. abort.
d S     M
Ms. Sterne < adv. abort.
d S     P
Ms. Sterne < Feminist

Note that in neither premise is the middle term distributed. Picturing the relationship of the terms in this syllogism, let a large open circle represent the undistributed term "those who advocate abortion." Place a smaller closed circle representing "all feminists" within the first circle. The minor premise then instructs us to place a circle representing Ms. Sterne within the circle representing those who advocate abortion. But where should the circle go since feminists do not cover the entire circle representing pro-abortionists? No conclusion is forced upon us. There are four possible relationships Ms. Sterne might have to the feminist group. She might be a member. She might not be a member. She might be in the process of becoming a member, or she might be canceling her membership. We have no way of knowing precisely about the relationship from the information given.

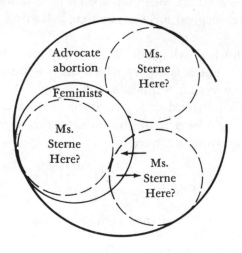

It should be noted that there is a second possible fallacy in this syllogism—the four-term fallacy. Ms. Sterne may advocate abortion in special cases but not on as wide a scale as resolutions of feminist groups generally propose. In the first premise we could have "advocates abortion upon any pregnant woman's request." In the second premise we could have "advocates abortion only in the case of rape or the prospect of a seriously deformed infant." That is, we would have four terms in the syllogism since those pertaining to abortion supply two different terms.

Recalling an earlier portion of our study, the *ad hominem* fallacy may be implicit in the thinking of the one proposing the initial argument: "Since Ms. Sterne is the sort of person who would advocate abortion, she must be the sort of person who would be a feminist."

Another instance of the fallacy of the undistributed middle might go like this. "All Christophers wear a St. Christopher's medal, and, since Benjie wears one, he must be a Christopher."

$$\begin{array}{ll} \text{d P} & \text{M} \\ \text{Christ.} < \text{wear St. C. medal.} \end{array}$$

$$\begin{array}{ll} \text{d S} & \text{M} \\ \text{Benjie} < \text{wear St. C. medal.} \end{array}$$

$$\begin{array}{ll} \text{d S} & \text{P} \\ \text{Benjie} < \text{Christ.} \end{array}$$

Diagramming this syllogism with circles results in uncertainty whether or not to place Benjie within the circle representing Christophers, just as in the preceding illustration instructions were not clear as to where to place Ms. Sterne with relation to feminists.

It might seem appropriate to supply an illustration of

the proper distribution to the middle term at this point. But such an illustration would be superflous here, for every valid syllogism is such an illustration, and a few valid syllogisms will be encountered in the exercises at the end of this chapter.

### d. *The Fallacy of Illicit Distribution*

For a categorical syllogism to be valid, a term distributed in the conclusion must be distributed in the premise in which it appears. To state the rule negatively: No term may be distributed in the conclusion if it is not distributed in a premise.

If the subject (minor) term is distributed in the conclusion, but not in the minor premise, the fallacy is said to be "illicit distribution of the minor term," or "illicit minor," for the sake of brevity. If the predicate (major) term is distributed in the conclusion but not in the major premise, the fallacy is called "illicit major," for short. Examine the following syllogism which appears at first to represent cogent reasoning.

All honest politicians shun large contributions.
All politicians who shun large contributions are impartial.
All politicians who are impartial are honest.

Note that "impartial politicians" is distributed in the conclusion, but not in the minor premise. Therefore we have the illicit distribution of the minor term.

Illustrating the syllogism with circles, let a middle-sized circle represent politicians who shun large contributions. Place within that circle a smaller circle representing all honest politicians. Now place the middle-sized circle with the smaller circle it contains within a large open circle representing the undistributed term, those who are impartial. It is obvious that there is ample room for someone to be impartial but still neither honest nor inclined to shun large contributions.

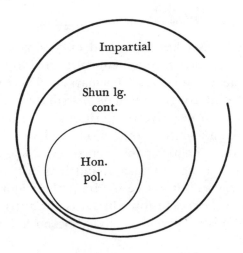

The following moderately attractive line of political persuasion abides by certain rules of the syllogism but is invalid because it commits the fallacy of illicit distribution of the major term: "Every newly elected congressman is limited to minor committee assignments. But Congressman

Taemarker is in the third term of his service and therefore not newly elected. So Congressman Taemarker will not be limited to minor committee asignments." Placing these terms in shortened form for clarity, we have:

$$
\begin{array}{ll}
\text{d M} & \text{P} \\
\text{Newly elect.} < \text{minor assgts.} \\
\text{d S} & \text{d M} \\
\text{Cong. Taem.} \not< \text{newly elect.} \\
\text{d S} & \text{d P} \\
\text{Cong. Taem.} \not< \text{minor assgts.}
\end{array}
$$

This syllogism has three and only three terms: newly elected congressmen, congressmen limited to minor assignments, and Congressman Taemarker. The middle term, newly elected congressmen, is distributed twice in fact. There are two negative propositions, with one of the exclusions being in the conclusion, and this is fine. The minor term, Congressman Taemarker, a singular term, is distributed in the conclusion, and it is distributed in the minor premise. But notice the flaw: the major term is distributed in the conclusion when it is not distributed in the major premise. Therefore, the syllogism is invalid.

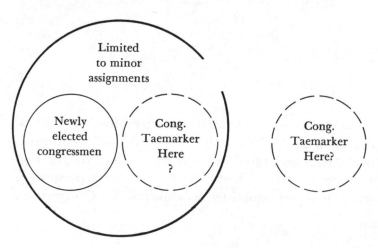

We can demonstrate that no conclusion is forced upon us by the use of circles. Let an open circle represent those congressmen limited to minor committee assignments. Place within this circle a closed circle representing "all newly elected congressmen." A third circle representing Congress Taemarker needs to be placed. But where should it go? All we know is that it must lie outside the circle representing the newly elected congressmen. (See diagram p. 156.)

e. *Two Special Cases*

There are two special cases regarding the categorical syllogism and these are discussed in Part III of the appendix. One of the cases involves the troublesome quantifier "most." "Most" certainly cannot be construed as "all." In most instances the quantifier must be interpreted as "some." However there arc cases where two "most" propositions appear in both the major and minor premises and in some of the arrangements a conclusion of "some" is possible.

The second special case pertains to the concept of the existential nature of certain propositions. It is important that students contemplating a more advanced course in logic examine this special case in the appendix.

Let us now examine the instances of syllogistic reasoning which introduced this chapter. The first commits the fallacy of the undistributed middle, for the term "those businesses which showed a profit" was not distributed in either premise.

The second commits two fallacies. One is the four-term fallacy. The first term is "those not engaged in marketing and management." The second term is "those who need to subscribe." The third term is "you." And the fourth term is "those engaged in marketing and management."

The second fallacy is that of the odd negative. The first premise is the only proposition stated negatively.

The third argument which seems to assure that refusing federal grants will mean no interference by the government commits the fallacy of illicit distribution of the major term. The term "regulation" is distributed in the conclusion but is not distributed in the major premise.

## EXERCISES: CHAPTER 7

Analyze the following for fallacies, and comment on the truth or reliability of the conclusions.

1. All laws have assigned penalties connected with them.
    Newton's conclusions concerning the mutual attraction of bodies have been stated as laws.
    Therefore, Newton's observations concerning the mutual attraction of bodies have assigned penalties connected with them.
2. All archaelogical artifacts are subject to Carbon 14 tests.
    The oil lamp Boyd found in the Palestinian tell is an archaeological artifact.
    Therefore the oil lamp is subject to Carbon 14 tests.
3. All good students like to read widely.
    Jan certainly likes to read widely.
    Therefore Jan is a good student.
4. All political party loyalists are swayed by their leader's speeches.
    No independent citizen is a political party loyalist.
    Therefore no independent citizen is swayed by a party leader's speeches.
5. All free enterprise advocates support a conservative party.
    All investors in stock favor "fair trade" pricing.

Therefore all investors in stocks support a conservative party.

6. No fundamentalist evangelist takes positions on sociopolitical issues.

    Some fundamentalist evangelists do not deviate from literal interpretations of the Bible.

    Thus, some who do not deviate from literal interpretations of the Bible take positions on sociopolitical issues.

7. Some men claim to be honest.

    No man is completely politically astute.

    Therefore some who are politically astute claim to be honest.

8. Most students who are partially or fully self-supporting take college work seriously.

    Ronnie certainly takes his college work seriously.

    It is evident that Ronnie is partially or fully self-supporting.

9. All education majors in the upper ten percent of their class are eligible for membership in Kappa Delta Pi.

    All commuting education majors are in the upper ten percent of their class.

    And so all commuting education majors are eligible for Kappa Delta Pi.

10. Some North Carolinians are Republicans.

    Most southeasterners are not Republicans.

    It follows, then, that some southeasterners are North Carolinians.

11. All politicians practice verbal sleight of hand.

    No concerned citizen practices verbal sleight of hand.

    So no concerned citizen is a politician.

12. All who fulfill their military commitments are patriotic.

All who fulfill their military commitments have stable home backgrounds.

We must conclude, then, that all who have stable home backgrounds are patriotic.

13. Some of the co-op foods were not perishable.

Most of the produce was perishable.

Therefore some of the produce was included in the co-op foods.

14. All who voted for Nixon had misgivings about McGovern.

Eric has made it perfectly clear that he had misgivings about McGovern.

Eric, I am sure, cast his vote for Nixon.

15. Agnew, upon resigning, entered a plea of *nolo contendere* as to the charges leveled against him.

*Nolo contendere* means "I do not contest the charges."

Agnew really, then, confesses to "guilty as charged."

16. All who use their knowledge of logic too freely irritate others.

Some logic students do use their knowledge of logic too freely.

Logic students surely do irritate others.

17. All seriously committed students spend considerable time in the library.

Some seniors are not seriously committed students.

So some seniors do not spend considerable time in the library.

18. Most bank directors are honest men.

The directors of our major local industry are members of the bank's board of directors.

The directors of our major local industry can be trusted as honest men.

*19. Slightly over half of those involved in varsity sports are physical education majors.

> Most of those involved in varsity sports receive some financial aid.
>
> So some of the physical education majors receive some financial aid.

20. Slightly over half of the physical education majors are involved in varsity sports.

> Most of those involved in varsity sports receive some financial aid.
>
> Therefore some of the physical education majors receive some sort of financial aid.

COMMENTS ON EXERCISES FOR CHAPTER 7

1. The four-term fallacy. In the major premise, "laws" means man-made laws in a judicial system. In the minor premise "laws" pertains to scientific principles.

2. Valid. This syllogism meets all of the tests to be applied to the categorical syllogism.

3. The fallacy of the undistributed middle. The middle term, "those who like to read widely," is not distributed in either premise.

4. The fallacy of illicit distribution of the major term. The predicate term of the conclusion, thus the major term "swayed by a party leader's speeches," is distributed in the conclusion but not distributed in the major premise.

5. The four-term fallacy. The terms are: 1. free enterprise advocates; 2. those who support a conservative party; 3. investors in stock; and 4. those who favor "fair trade" pricing.

---

*See Part III of the appendix before considering 19 and 20.

6. The fallacy of the odd negative. There is an even number of negatives but they are oddly placed. They are both in the premises and thus do not permit the premises to yield a conclusion.

7. The odd negative. There is only one negative proposition and it is in the minor premise.

8. The undistributed middle. The term, "those who take college work seriously," is not distributed in either premise.

9. Valid. The addition of "commuting" to "education majors" does not make a fourth term for they are still education majors.

10. The odd negative. Only the minor premise contains a negative. This is an instance in which we know both premises and the conclusion to be true. But their truth is based upon experience. The syllogism itself is invalid.

11. Valid. The reliability of the conclusion might be called into question for it would be very difficult to demonstrate the truth of the premises.

12. Illicit minor. "Those who have stable home backgrounds" is the minor term and is distributed in the conclusion but not in the minor premise.

13. The odd negative. Only the major premise contains a negative.

14. The undistributed middle.

15. The four-term fallacy. *Nolo contendere,* some say, is Latin for "guilty as hell." This is a psychological construction put upon this legal practice. The strict translation, "I do not wish to contend," establishes neither guilt nor innocence, logically speaking.

16. The conclusion in this syllogism is a vague proposition. If it is rendered, "Some logic students . . . irritate

others," the syllogism is valid. If it is rendered, "All logic students . . . irritate others," the minor term has been illicitly distributed.

17. Illicit major.
18. The minor premise is a vague proposition. Whether it is restated, "All of the directors" or "Some of the directors," does not really matter. In each case there would still be a fallacy, that of the undistributed middle.
19. Valid.
20. Invalid. It can be shown by diagrams, preferably rectangles, that there is no forced overlapping of physical education majors and those receiving financial assistance. Or this can be demonstrated by some simple arithmetic. Suppose there are 10 physical education majors and 6 of them ("slightly over half") are involved in varsity sports. Suppose there are 50 involved in varsity sports, 40 of whom receive financial aid. Some or all of the 6 physical education majors who are involved in varsity sports may be within the 40 receiving financial aid or some or all of the 6 may be in the group of 10 varsity sports participants receiving no financial aid.

# Chapter 8

# Clarifying Vague Propositions

Some of the sections of the preceding chapters emphasized that clear thinking requires first, the use of words which are clear and agreed upon as to meaning by both speaker and hearer or writer and reader, and second, the stating of a proposition so that the subject is clearly related to the predicate in one way and in one way only.

Our conversation and writing would be rendered dull and prosaic if we used only sentences appropriate in their structure to the canons of logic. But to convey logical thoughts our conversation and writing must be reducible to such modes of expression. Ambiguous or vague statements must be capable of being expressed in terms of inclusion in or exclusion from certain categories. Logic deals largely with such inclusion or exclusion. This has clearly been the case in working with the categorical syllogism.

So now, before we proceed with other forms of syllogistic reasoning, we shall analyze some typical vague statements and how they are to be expressed in strict logical form. Strict logical form in the case of the categorical syllogism requires definite quantifiers, "all" or "some," and explicit exclusion or inclusion in the relationship between terms. The hypothetical, alternative and disjunctive forms come up later.

We must restate for logical clarity many statements like the following:

| | |
|---|---|
| 1. "Few . . . are . . ." | 6. "All but . . . are . . ." |
| 2. "A few . . . are . . ." | 7. "None but . . . are . . ." |
| 3. "All . . . are not . . ." | 8. "Only . . . are. . ." |
| 4. ". . . are . . ." | 9. ". . . alone are . . ." |
| 5. "Not all . . . are . . ." | 10. "Unless . . ." |

In these statements the verb "are" is used, but many other verbs may appear instead of forms of the verb to be: "make," "do," "use," "believe," etc., to an indefinitely large list.

1 AND 2. "FEW . . . ARE . . ." AND "A FEW . . . ARE . . ."

"Few . . . are . . ." translates into "Some . . . are not . . ." while "A few . . . are . . ." translates into "Some . . . are. . . ."

If you say, "Few politicians are honest," you probably have the somber notion in mind that "Most politicians are not honest." The statement might possibly be interpreted as meaning, of course, that "A few politicians are honest." But if the latter meaning is intended the statement should be in the logical form, "Some politicians are honest." This is more than a matter of convenience in logical discourse. It is necessary.

"Few . . . are . . ." generally appears to mean, "Some . . . are not. . . ." "Few migrant workers have adequate retirement benefits" means "Some migrant workers do not have adequate retirement benefits." In this case the original statement probably means that "most migrant workers do not have adequate retirement benefits." But, "most" is rarely usable in logical propositions, as we have seen.

"A few ... are ..." means "Some ... are. ..."

"A few voters approved the school lunch program" means that one knows that in a certain election some of the voters did approve the school lunch program. In strict logical form this would read, "Some voters are included in those who approved the school lunch program." It may have been that only a minority of the voters approved the program. Of course a majority, or even all, of the voters may have approved the program. But, the one making the initial statement has revealed no more than knowledge of part of the vote count. Similarly, "A few voters are members of a third party" means, "Some voters are included in members of a third party."

### 3. "All . . . are not . . . "

"All ... are not ..." translates into "Some ... are not ..." simply because that is the customary interpretation of such a proposition. "All Vietnam veterans are not drug addicts" would ordinarily be accepted as meaning, "Some Vietnam veterans are not drug addicts." While a strictly literal interpretation of the expression could mean that "All Vietnam veterans are excluded from those who are drug addicts," reliable information, tragically enough, contradicts such a statement. In a statement conforming to what we know to be the case and at the same time suitable to logical analysis, then, the proposition should be, "Some Vietnam veterans are excluded from those who are drug addicts."

"All blacks are not happy about the progress of civil rights during the past decade" does not, one hopes, mean that "All blacks are dissatisfied with the progress of civil rights during the past decade." As a matter of fact, one can document the assertion that "Some blacks are satisfied with the progress of civil rights. . . ." When we recall our experience with syllogistic analysis the necessity for stating explicitly such propositions as we are now considering should be fully apparent. In this instance, the statement "All blacks are not happy about the progress of civil rights" should be restated, "Some blacks are excluded from those who are happy about the progress of civil rights. . . ."

### 4. "... ARE ..." (STATEMENTS WITHOUT QUANTIFIERS)

A statement without any quantifier at all presents special difficulties. Logical discourse requires that a quantifier be suppied. If a speaker or writer does not fulfill this obligation, the listener or reader can only reconstruct an expression lacking a quantifier as best he can from its context. A conservative interpretation is recommended for in logic the acceptance of a conclusion requires that it be forced.

"Porpoises are more intelligent than sharks" may mean for the ichthyologist that "All porpoises are more intelligent than sharks in general." We would be more comfortable, however, if the quantifier were expressed.

Some statements by their nature, as is usually the case with definitions, imply "all." "Bachelors are unmarried men" means "All bachelors are unmarried men" by the customary definition of the word "bachelor." A problem arises, however, in regard to many sentences. What does "Blessed are the meek" mean? Does it mean, "All who are blessed are included among the meek"? Or does it mean, "All who are meek are included among the blessed"? Or does it mean that "Some of the blessed are meek," or that

"Some of the meek are blessed"? One might hope that an equivalence of the terms is the case, but how can one be certain?

It would be a bit risky to interpret the following sentences as meaning "All . . . are. . . ." "Professors are absentminded." "Good citizens contribute to a political party." "Those who contribute to a political party are civic minded." "Freshmen are wild because of newfound freedom." "Veterans are militarists." Certainly in these and many such cases the proper construction is to be made as "Some . . . are. . . ."

## 5. "NOT ALL . . . ARE . . ."

"Not all . . . are . . ." is to be interpreted as "Some are not. . . ."

"Not all Vietnam veterans are drug addicts" is properly construed as "Some Vietnam veterans are not drug addicts." Remember from the discussion of conversion and obversion that this statement should not be interpreted as meaning that "Some Vietnam veterans are drug addicts." This appears from published reports, alas, to be true. But the last statement cannot be derived from the initial form. Similarly, "Not all men with long hair are antiestablishment" means "Some men with long hair are not antiestablishment."

## 6. "ALL BUT . . . ARE . . ."

Statements expressed in terms of "All but . . ." and "All except . . ."

are rather troublesome and the construction to be put upon statements of this kind can arouse debate very easily. "All but (except) Jim passed the course" may allow, some will claim, for the fact that it is not known at the time of the statement whether or not Jim passed the course. Others will claim with some fervor that the statement means that Jim did not pass the course and that he was the only one who did not pass the course. To settle such a dispute two statements may be made. If it is not known whether Jim was among those passing the course, the statements would read "All students-other-than-Jim passed the course," and "It is not known whether Jim passed the course."

If it is known that Jim did not pass the course and it is important to be precise about the situation regarding Jim and his fellow students, the two assertions would go thus: "All students-other-than-Jim passed the course" and "Jim did not pass the course."

Fortunately exceptive statements usually are descriptive of a situation, informative about conclusions already reached, rather than premises in an argument. But they do appear and we must cope with them. We will therefore examine one more of the interpretations sometimes put upon the "All but . . ." or "All except . . ." type of statement. This is the view that the intent of such statements seems to be to exclude some specified group and to include another.

For example, "All but those who attend class regularly will fail to earn high grades" does not mean that those who attend regularly will earn high grades. The work may be beyond their competence regardless of their faithfulness in attendance. The statement merely excludes those with poor attendance from those who earn high grades. The strict form of such a statement would be, "All who do not attend class regularly are excluded from those who earn high grades." The same sort of revised wording would apply to "All except . . ." of course.

## 7. "None but . . . are . . ."

"None but . . ." or "None except . . ."

propositions present similar difficulties to those encountered in the preceding paragraphs. Customarily, "None but (or except) Jim passed the course" implies that Jim passed the course but no one else did. However, the pettifogger might insist that the "None but (or except) . . ." wording still leaves room for the fact that Jim failed to pass the course too. He would say that the statement does not clearly tell us that Jim actually passed the course. Again this form of proposition requires considerable reconstruction to fit into syllogistic form.

For clarification it may be helpful to move from a single exception to a group exclusion. Let us use the illustration, "None but early risers tolerate reveille with good humor." If the proposition is true, and this supposition must underlie our illustrations if they are to be useful, the fact is, "All who tolerate reveille with good humor are early risers." It does not mean, "All early risers tolerate reveille with good humor." Many early risers may be irritated that the morning bugle call interrupted something they arose early to do.

Again, "None but the brave deserve the fair" is to be construed as "All who deserve the fair are brave." The interpretation "All the brave deserve the fair" is inappropriate, for some of the brave may be disqualified by some other factors not included in the intent of the statement. But, if one is deserving of the fair, then he is certainly included in the larger class of the brave. Compare such kinds of statements with those discussed next.

## 8. "Only . . . are . . ."

"Only . . . are . . ."

statements require a sort of conversion. "Only students with ID cards will be admitted to the concert free of charge" does not mean that all students with ID cards will actually be admitted. The statement means rather that if the management sticks to the regulation and if there are no gatecrashers, "All of those admitted free have ID cards." "Only those with fishing licenses may fish in this stream" means that "All who fish in this stream have, or should have, fishing licenses." The original statement does not mean that "All who have fishing licenses may fish in this stream." The stream may be inaccessible to some. Others may have the license but not the proper form of bait. Or some may have a license but not fulfil some additional requirement for the particular area in which the stream is located.

## 9. ". . . ALONE ARE . . ."

". . . alone are . . ." has essentially the same meaning as

"only . . . are. . . ."

"Those alone who have ID cards may attend the concert without charge" does not mean to exclude dating couples although an overly strict application of the wording as it stands would mean just that. "Those alone who have donated fifty dollars to the ecology program will be listed as patrons" does not exclude a man and his wife from being listed as joint donors. In strict logical form such statements as these would be rendered: "All those who attend this concert without charge are included in those who have ID cards," and "All those who are listed as patrons of this ecology program are included in those who have donated fifty dollars to the program."

## 10. "UNLESS . . ."

The treatment of statements beginning with "unless" is similar to those involving "alone." "Unless a man is born again he cannot enter the kingdom of heaven" means, "Only men who are born again can enter the kingdom of heaven." This in turn, of course, means, "All who can enter the kingdom of heaven are included in those who have been born again." The original statement may have been intended to indicate that all the reborn may qualify for entrance into the kingdom, but that is not what it says in any usable logical sense. And, indeed, some theologians would insist this could not have been its original meaning since some who have been reborn (whatever that means) might do something to nullify their chances of gaining entrance to the kingdom of heaven.

### EXERCISES: CHAPTER 8

Restate the following in strict logical form.
1. All but those majoring in French may take the course "French Literature in Translation."
2. A few of the industrial arts products for the benefit sale turned out to be virtually flawless.
3. Few students of logic boast that a study of logic will solve all of their problems.
4. Unless one applies for the humanities grant by October 1, his application will not be considered.
5. All advertisements are not informative and factual.
6. Students who have a 3.0 quality point ratio for three successive quarters may enroll for a three quarter-hour overload.
7. Only students who have a 3.0 quality point ratio for three successive quarters may enroll for a three quarter-hour overload.

8. Only the thrifty can balance their budgets.
9. Dictatorships employ force and suppress freedom of speech and press.
10. Not all college professors are absentminded.
11. All college professors are not absentminded.
12. Everyone should not go to college.
13. Wise are they who plan with care for the future.
14. Few housewives are unconcerned about inflation.
15. Cattle raisers who withheld their steers from the market in recent weeks are now faced with lower prices.
16. None but students who have at least 2.0 quality point ratios may take part in intercollegiate athletics.
17. Politicians are dishonest.
18. A few advertisements are factual and informative.
19. Election irregularities will continue to trouble the country unless detailed corrective legislation is designed and enacted.
20. A columnist who had followed the career of Wapsly from courthouse to congress cautioned, "All that Wapsly says is not true."

### COMMENTS ON EXERCISES FOR CHAPTER 8

1. A statement like this in a college catalog is probably intended to exclude French majors from taking the course in question. However, a strict logical interpretation of the wording would result in this form: "All non-French majors are included in those who may take the course 'French Literature in Translation.' "
2. Some of the industrial arts products for the benefit sale are included in those that turned out to be virtually flawless.
3. Some students of logic are excluded from those that boast that a study of logic will solve all of their problems.

4. All who do not apply for the humanities grant by October 1 will be excluded from those whose applications will be considered. It is important to note that this statement does not guarantee that those who do apply before the deadline will have their applications considered.

5. Some advertisements are excluded from things that are informative and factual. The original statement does not say that some advertisements are informative and factual but it leaves room for that possibility.

6. The statement is probably to be construed as allowing all students who have at least a 3.0 quality point ratio, etc., to enroll for a three quarter-hour overload. But, this is the sort of regulation that does need more careful wording and the inclusion of a quantifier.

7. All students who may enroll for a three quarter-hour overload are included in students who have at least a 3.0 quality point ratio for three successive quarters. This allows for the exclusion of some such students on other grounds, such as the level of their courses, the content of certain courses, etc.

8. All who can balance their budgets are thrifty. Neither statement may be true, of course, for some who are wealthy may not need to be thrifty in order to balance their budgets. But, if the original statement is true, the revised wording would be its proper logical form.

9. By the usual concept of dictatorship this statement may mean, "All dictatorships employ force. . . ." But the need for a quantifier is clear for this to be in strict logical form.

10. Some college professors are excluded from the absent-minded.

11. Some college professors are excluded from the absent-minded. The answers to both 10 and 11 conform with the customary interpretation.

12. Some persons are excluded from those who should go to college. Certainly one making the original statement does not mean to close college doors by having his assertion interpreted, "All individuals should refrain from going to college."

13. This statement is so ambiguous that the writer or speaker should phrase it more carefully. He has a choice. Does he mean, "All who are wise are included in those who prepare for the future"? Or does he mean, "All of those who prepare for the future are included in the wise"?

14. Some housewives are excluded from those who are unconcerned about inflation. It is likely that all housewives are not unconcerned (are concerned) about inflation. But at least some are not unconcerned (are concerned) about inflation.

15. One offering the judgment should specify whether all cattleraisers are to be included in those facing lower prices, or just some cattleraisers.

16. All who may take part in intercollegiate athletics are included in those who have at least 2.0 quality point ratios. The original statement does not assure that a 2.0 quality point ratio will justify a position in intercollegiate sports. That is, it does not state, "All who have at least 2.0 quality point ratios are included in those who may take part in intercollegiate sports."

17. A cynical person may mean, "All politicians are included in dishonest persons." But the statement does require quantifying to be acceptable in a line of reasoning.

18. Some advertisements are included in things that are factual and informative.

19. If detailed corrective legislation is not designed and enacted, election irregularities will continue, etc. This statement can be framed in categorical form thus:

"All instances in which detailed corrective legislation is not designed and enacted are included in instances where election irregularities will continue." Unhappily neither statement assures that enacting corrective legislation will result in eliminating election irregularities.

20. Some things that Wapsly says are excluded from things that are true.

# Chapter 9

# The Hypothetical Syllogism

"If you want more taxes, more government expenditures, and more government controls, then vote for my opponent. But you certainly do not want more taxes, expenditures and controls. And so I ask for your vote." So goes a typical and frequently effective political appeal. But the argument has a serious fault. The candidate has broken a very important rule governing the hypothetical syllogism. What is it?

"If we are to avoid a serious confrontation with Russia then we must match or exceed her in military strength. Our military strength exceeds hers and therefore we are going to avoid a serious confrontation." This line of thought, so comforting to so many, is also flawed. In what respect?

Unlike the categorical proposition, which makes a direct assertion, the hypothetical proposition is a supposition, an assumption. For those interested in etymology, "hypothesis" is formed from two Greek words: *hypo*, meaning "under", and *tithenai* meaning "to put." So when we hypothesize, we put one idea under another, or undergird a term with a supposition.

Sometimes hypotheses are specifically expressed, and sometimes they are implied. "If Nixon had lost the 1972 election, the country would not have been disturbed by a Watergate-type incident" is an expressed hypothetical statement. "A hit dog always hollers" is a categorical proposition which implies a hypothetical notion, for it means, "If a dog is hit it will holler."

The proposition about Nixon's election commits the fallacy we considered earlier known as the hypothesis contrary to fact. Furthermore, if we place it in syllogistic form, adding a minor premise and a conclusion, we will see an instance of an invalid hypothetical syllogism.

> If Nixon had lost the 1972 election then the country would not have been disturbed by a Watergate-type incident.
> Nixon did not lose the 1972 election.
> Therefore . . .

No conclusion whatever is possible. The fallacy is that the minor premise denies the antecedent, the part of the proposition following the "if." The fact that Watergate did occur does not mean that a conclusion of any kind can be reached from these premises.

If Nixon had lost the election, the minor premise would then affirm the antecedent, and the conclusion, "The country would not have been disturbed by a Watergate-type incident," would then be valid. The conclusion would be unreliable, however, for it is conceivable that some Watergate-type incident could have occurred. In fact, the Watergate incident occurred quite some time before the election. If he had lost the election, Nixon might have been involved in curious legal tangles involving what investigators and courts should do concerning an ex-president allegedly involved in questionable pursuits. Note the cautious use of the wording "might have been." This is an attempt to avoid committing a further fallacy in dealing with the hypothetical while trying to explain what the syllogism involves.

Compare the previous syllogism with a very easily manageable one.

> Major premise: If it rains the sidewalk will be wet.
> Minor premise: It has not rained.
> Conclusion: The sidewalk will not be wet.

Obviously the sidewalk can be wet without its having rained. Snow may have melted on it. Someone may have decided to hose it down. The street department may have feared it would become icy and so sprinkled it with calcium chloride which absorbed enough water to dampen it.

The categorical syllogism has very few rules one must keep in mind while checking it for validity. The hypothetical syllogism has even fewer, only two. Some authors in the area of logic nonethless develop longer chapters on the hypothetical syllogism and its variations than on the categorical syllogism. They do this by developing a variety of patterns and tables pertaining to implication and by converting categorical propositions into hypothetical propositions. Such conversion is sometimes useful in carefully checking out a line of reasoning and we will develop the procedure later. At this point let us consider the two rules governing the hypothetical syllogism and the corollary of each rule.

## 1. RULE ONE AND COROLLARY

Rule 1: The minor premise of a hypothetical syllogism may affirm, but may not negate or deny, the antecedent of the major premise.

Corollary: When the antecedent is affirmed in the minor premise, the conclusion must follow through by affirming the consequent of the major premise.

We have examined what happens when the minor premise denies the antecedent of the major premise. Now note what happens when the minor premise affirms the antecedent but the conclusion does not follow through by affirming the consequent.

If an accurate thermometer registers an above normal reading, then I have an elevation in temperature.
This is an accurate thermometer and it registers an above normal reading.
But I have no elevation in temperature.

Clearly there is something wrong here. We would judge it to be either that the thermometer was not accurate, or that I just would not admit having an elevation in temperature. We would accept the following pattern readily, however.

If an accurate thermometer registers an above normal reading, then I have an elevation in temperature.
This is an accurate thermometer, and it registers an above normal reading.
So I have an elevation in temperature.

The conclusion meets the conditions of the corollary to the first rule by affirming the consequent, and so the syllogism is valid. The argument is also sound, leading to a reliable conclusion, since the premises are true and related in a valid fashion.

## 2. RULE TWO AND COROLLARY

Rule 2: The minor premise may deny or negate but may not affirm, the consequent of the major premise.

Corollary: When the consequent is denied in the minor premise, the conclusion must follow through by denying or negating the antecedent.

First let us give a simple illustration of the proper or valid procedure in observing this rule and its corollary. Again, rain and wet sidewalks will serve.

> If it rains the sidewalk will be wet.
> The sidewalk is not wet.
> Therefore it has not rained.

Let us use to illustrate an invalid hypothetical argument one based on the old aphorism, "A hit dog always hollers." This usually means that if someone sharply criticizes another person and the criticism is met either with obvious embarrassment or with a very strong objection then the criticism is valid. The aphorism should be stated in strict logical form thus:

> If a dog is hit, it will holler.
> That dog hollered.
> Therefore that dog was hit.

Despite the frequency with which we encounter this old saw, its implications when logically expressed and examined will clearly be shown to be invalid. This syllogism violates Rule 2 governing the hypothetical syllogism, the rule that the minor premise leads to no forced conclusion when it affirms the consequent of the major premise. The minor premise must deny the consequent if a conclusion is to be reached.

It is the case, of course, that dogs will holler for many more reasons than being hit, just as the sidewalk in an earlier illustration can be wet from other sources than rain. If we accepted the usual line of thought regarding hollering dogs, we could never respond to any criticism no matter how unfair and unfounded. Responding to criticism in and of itself becomes substantiation of the criticism.

Regarding the various forms of syllogistic reasoning, it should be kept in mind that truth, validity and reliability are all involved in any useful or, as some prefer to put it, sound forms of logical reasoning. In the case of the hypothetical syllogism, as with other types of syllogisms, premises must be true, they must be related in a valid way, and the conclusion must follow through properly for the conclusion to be reliable.

### 3. A SPECIAL CASE OF THE HYPOTHETICAL SYLLOGISM

Sometimes one states an "if . . . then . . ." when more strictly speaking he should say, "If and only if . . . then. . . ." For example, "If today is Friday, tomorrow will be Saturday" means, by the fixed arrangement of days of the week, "If and only if today is Friday will tomorrow be Saturday." It is unlikely one will commit an error in developing a syllogism based upon this particular proposition. One rather automatically affirms the antecedent and then affirms the consequent:

> If today is Friday, tomorrow will be Saturday.
> Today is Friday.
> Therefore tomorrow will be Saturday.

Or one denies the antecedent and then denies the consequent:

> If today is Friday, tomorrow will be Saturday.
> Today is not Friday.
> Therefore tomorrow will not be Saturday.

Or one affirms the consequent and then affirms the antecedent:

> If today is Friday, tomorrow will be Saturday.
> Tomorrow will be Saturday.
> Therefore today is Friday.

Or one denies the consequent and then denies the antecedent:

> If today is Friday, tomorrow will be Saturday.
> Tomorrow will not be Saturday.
> Therefore today is not Friday.

The earlier rules against denying the antecedent and affirming the consequent do not apply, as we see, to the "If and only if . . . then . . ." proposition.

With the hypothetical, as with other types of syllogistic reasoning, a syllogism may be valid or invalid quite independently of whether the contents of their premises have any meaning. We do not need to know whether or not nexxos, whisbies and tiddledums exist to defend the validity of the following syllogism:

> If a nexxo is a whisbie, it is a tiddledum.
> This nexxo is a whisbie.
> Therefore this nexxo is a tiddledum.

Since the minor premise affirms the antecedent and the conclusion affirms the consequent, the syllogism is valid. Whether the conclusion is reliable or not we do not know. Similarly:

> If a nexxo is a whisbie, it is a tiddledum.
> This nexxo is not a tiddledum.
> Therefore this nexxo is not a whisbie.

The conclusion is valid. Whether the conclusion is true and reliable or whether the argument is sound, we cannot know until we know what nexxo, whisbie and tiddledum represent and whether the propositions about them are true.

## 4. The Conversion of Syllogistic Forms

While some purists in the field of logic object to rephrasing categorical syllogisms in hypothetical form, and vice versa, on the grounds that the categorical syllogism deals with the relationship of propositions and the hypothetical syllogism with the relationship of terms, careful rephrasing does no violence to logical principles in any practical sense and sometimes reassures one in the analysis of a syllogism. It is necessary to change the wording, obviously, but the procedure is simple. Let us consider rain and wet sidewalks again.

> If it rains, the sidewalk will be wet.
> It has rained.
> Therefore the sidewalk is wet.

This becomes, in categorical form:

> All instances in which it rains are included in instances in which the sidewalk will be wet.
> This is an instance when it has rained.
> Therefore, this is an instance in which the sidewalk will be wet.

One may convert the categorical form into the hypothetical form. Let us use as an example the following categorical syllogism:

> All crows are black.
> This bird is a crow.
> Therefore this bird is black.

This syllogism becomes, in hypothetical form:

> If a bird is a crow, it is black.
> This bird is a crow.
> Therefore this bird is black.

It is of interest to note some patterns that develop in

restating syllogisms in another form. The fallacy of affirming the consequent in the hypothetical is equivalent to the fallacy of the undistributed middle in the categorical syllogism.

Compare two syllogisms involving the yelping dog.

> If a dog is hit, it will holler.
> This dog hollered.
> Therefore this dog was hit.

The fallacy of affirming the consequent has been committed as we have already noted. Now examine the same in categorical form.

$$\begin{array}{cc} \text{d P} & \text{M} \end{array}$$
Instances dog hit $<$ instances dog will holler.
$$\begin{array}{cc} \text{d S} & \text{M} \end{array}$$
This instance $<$ instances of dog hollering.
$$\begin{array}{cc} \text{d S} & \text{P} \end{array}$$
This instance $<$ dog being hit.

The fallacy of denying the antecedent in the hypothetical syllogism turns out to be the equivalent of the fallacy of illicit major in handling the categorical syllogism. The following illustrates this equivalence.

> If it rains, the sidewalk will be wet.
> It has not rained.
> Therefore, the sidewalk is not wet.

The minor premise denies the antecedent and so the syllogism is not valid. Now for the categorical form.

$$\begin{array}{cc} \text{d M} & \text{P} \end{array}$$
Instances of rain $<$ sidewalk wet.
$$\begin{array}{cc} \text{d S} & \text{d M} \end{array}$$
This instance $\not<$ instances of rain.
$$\begin{array}{cc} \text{d S} & \text{d P} \end{array}$$
Therefore this instance $\not<$ instances of sidewalk wet.

## 5. Symbols for Use with the Hypothetical Syllogism

It is convenient to use two symbols for abbreviating hypothetical propositions. A horseshoe open to the left, $\supset$, symbolizes the basic "If . . . then . . ." while three parallel lines, $\equiv$, often used to indicate identity, denote "If and only if . . . then. . . ." Or two sidewise horseshoes may be used for "If and only if . . . then . . ."

Thus illustrations used earlier in this chapter could be represented in a sort of logic shorthand and with helpful clarity as follows.

The one regarding Nixon's election and Watergate would appear:

> Lost elect. $\supset$ no W. prob.
> — lose elect.
> — W. prob. (Inv. D.A.)

Regarding the days of the week:

> Today Fri. $\equiv$ tom. Sat. (or $\supset \supset$)
> Fri.
> Tom. Sat. (Val.)

Note:
1. Various words other than "if . . . then . . ." are used to express hypothetical statements: when, had, etc. "When strip mining is excessive the environment suffers." "Had the adverse effects of oxygen on premature babies' eyes been known in the 1950s, caution in its use would have been indicated."
2. Frequently the "if" portion of the hypothetical statement will be in the latter part of the proposition. "Soil is much more productive if it is tested and fertilized according to needs that tests show." In such instances one needs to keep in mind that the antecedent term is the one following the stated or implied

"if," and the consequent is the term in the proposition following the stated or implied "then."

What, then, were the fallacies in reasoning involved in the illustrations which introduced this chapter? The political candidate has denied the antecedent in his hypothetical statement. "If you want more taxes, etc., vote for my opponent," he said. "But you do not want more taxes, etc.," denies or negates the antecedent and renders the argument invalid.

Those taking comfort in thinking that we are exceeding Russia in military strength and that this will, on the basis of the argument presented, avoid a confrontation with Russia have committed the fallacy of affirming the consequent. Even if we accept the premise that equality with or outpacing Russia militarily will guarantee avoidance of a confrontation, the reasoning is unsound. Much more, it is reasonable to assume, must be done to perpetuate detente or gain eventual cooperation than merely to tie or win in an arms race.

## EXERCISES: CHAPTER 9

Examine the following for fallacies. Convert those not in hypothetical form to that form. Comment upon the reliability of the conclusions.

1. If anything is fair, it is honorable.
   That stewardess surely is fair.
   Therefore she must be honorable.
2. If one is a child he is innocent.
   Roscoe is no longer a child.
   Therefore Roscoe is not innocent.
3. If Kennedy and King were alive today, social progress would be assured.
   But, they are not alive.
   Therefore social progress is by no means assured.

4. If our theory is correct, our experiments will work.
   Our experiments have worked beautifully.
   Therefore our theory is correct.

5. If our experiments work out satisfactorily, our theory
   will be proved correct.
   Our experiments have all worked out satisfactorily.
   Therefore our theory is correct.

6. If one is a political liberal, he will favor increased
   governmental and economic planning.
   Wallace is not a political liberal.
   Therefore Wallace will object to increased governmental and economic planning.

7. If the reports on Ethiopian difficulties are true, Selas-
   sie will have to change his policy.
   The reports have been carefully verified as true.
   Therefore Selassie will have to change his policy.

8. If the reports on Ethiopian difficulties are true, Selassie will have to change his policy.
   Selassie insists he will not change his policy and so
   will not.
   Therefore the reports are not true.

9. If anyone could travel at the speed of light, he could
   theoretically live forever.
   Man's mind can travel at the speed of light.
   Therefore man's mind can theoretically live forever.

10. If one is not for us, he is against us.
    He is for us.
    Therefore he is not against us.

11. If a proposition applies to all members of a class, it
    is a "universal" proposition.
    "All metals are elements" is a universal proposition.
    Therefore "All metals are elements" applies to all
    members of a class.

12. When a union demand is granted, it is followed by an inflationary spiral.

     The union demand this time was denied.

     Thus we will not be facing an inflationary spiral.

13. Dangerous radioactive material is spread in the atmosphere and food supplies when atomic test explosions are conducted.

     We have discontinued such tests.

     Therefore radioactive material will not be further spread in the atmosphere and in food supplies.

14. "I will abide by the constitution," President Nixon said, "if the congressional judicial committee does."

     The congressional judicial committee has scrupulously abided by the constitution.

     Therefore President Nixon will do the same.

15. Grover Cleveland's illegitimate son would surely have been an insurmountable political handicap had his existence been made known to the public.

     Cleveland's opponents used publicity about the "natural son" against Cleveland.

     And so it was that Cleveland was defeated.

16. When a man is candidate for high office, his personal affairs properly become the concern of the electorate.

     Kennedy's personal affairs are no one's business.

     Therefore Kennedy is not a candidate for high office.

17. All nations that are firmly friendly and democratic may expect the United States to trade with them on a favorable basis.

     Russia is deficient in both firm friendliness and democratic practices.

     So Russia is certain to be denied favorable trade terms.

18. I cannot work at maximum efficiency when my type-writer needs adjustments and cleaning.
    I am not working at maximum efficiency today.
    It must be that my typewriter needs adjustments and cleaning.

19. If the transmission needs overhauling, my car will perform very sluggishly.
    That's precisely the way it's performing, sluggishly.
    So I suppose it needs a transmission overhaul.

20. If I am to win this game, I must be dealt a good hand.
    Aha! A good hand!
    I'm bound to win, so I am going to raise the stakes.

### COMMENTS ON EXERCISES FOR CHAPTER 9

1. The four-term fallacy. This fallacy applies to the various forms of the syllogism. "Fair" in the major premise is used in the sense of just, or equitable. In the minor premise, "fair" has to do with attractive physical qualities.

2. Invalid. The minor premise denies the antecedent. If this syllogism were transposed into categorical form, the fallacy would be that of illicit major.

$$
\begin{array}{ll}
\text{d M} & \text{P} \\
\text{Children} < \text{innocent.} \\
\text{d S} & \text{d M} \\
\text{Roscoe} \not< \text{children.} \\
\text{d S} & \text{d P} \\
\text{Roscoe} \not< \text{innocent.}
\end{array}
$$

3. Invalid. The antecedent is denied. Note also that the hypothesis contrary to fact is involved.

4. Invalid. The minor premise affirms the consequent. If transposed into categorical form, the fallacy of the undistributed middle is committed.

5.  Valid. But, doubtful as to the reliability or soundness of the argument. The major premise is subject to question, for still further experiments may not be successful.

6.  Invalid. The antecedent is denied.

7.  Valid. However, as historical developments turned out, Selassie did not actually change the policy at issue when this syllogism was composed and was subsequently divested of his authority.

8.  Valid. But, unreliable, as developments revealed.

9.  Valid as to form. The major premise is subject to serious question, and the equivalence of the terms "anyone" and "man's mind" is not certain.

10.  Invalid. The minor premise denies the antecedent. This is an illustration of the fact that the various propositions of a syllogism may be accepted as true while the line of argument itself is invalid. Furthermore, the major premise commits the black-or-white fallacy. One who is "not for us" may be neutral and not necessarily against us. Some would interpret this as a case of strong alternation (an "either . . . or . . . but not both" proposition) parading in hypothetical disguise. "Strong alternation" will be considered in Chapter 10.

11.  Invalid. The consequent is affirmed. And yet, the conclusion would be accepted as true by definition, or by conventional usage of the terms.

12.  Invalid. The minor premise denies the antecedent, the term following the "when," which implies "if."

13.  Invalid. The minor premise denies the antecedent. However, the invalidity of the form of this argument should not lead one to favor atomic test explosions, for this is another instance where matters of truth and validity do not happen to coincide.

14. Valid. Of course, events as they developed reveal the lack of reliability in the argument.
15. Valid. Actually, Cleveland was elected, indicating again that valid reasoning is not always sound.
16. Valid. But, reliability or soundness of the argument needs some examination.
17. Invalid. The antecedent is denied in the minor premise. In hypothetical form this syllogism would read:

> Friendly, demo. ⊃ fav. trade.
> — Russia friendly, demo.
> — Russia fav. trade.

18. Invalid. The consequent is affirmed in the hypothetical form or the syllogism.

> Need adj. ⊃ not work. eff.
> Not work. eff.
> Need adj.

19. Invalid. The consequent has been affirmed. The automobile should be checked to see if some lesser expense such as a tune-up might be involved.
20. Invalid. Again, the consequent has been affirmed. A good hand of cards must still be played properly to assure a win.

# Chapter 10

# Alternatives and Disjunctives in Syllogistic Reasoning

We daily encounter choices, alternatives, and "either . . . or . . ." situations. "Francine has either influenza or mononucleosis." "Is it Nat's fault or Nancy's that they are being divorced?" "Either the electricity is off or there is something wrong with my dishwasher." "Spelvin is low on quality points, so he's either lazy or not prepared for college work." "We will have either freedom or regimentation." "Let's see, now. It's either Tuesday or Wednesday."

Consider Francine's situation. "Francine has either influenza or mononucleosis." May she not be unfortunate enough to have both influenza *and* mononucleosis? Think about Nat and Nancy for a moment. "Is it Nat's fault or Nancy's that they are being divorced?" May they not both be at fault? Is it possible that neither is at fault? So too with the statement, "Either the electricity is off or there is something wrong with my dishwasher." The electricity may be off *and* the dishwasher out of order.

But with "We will have either freedom or regimentation," there is presented a different sort of alternative situation. "It is either Tuesday or Wednesday" also represents a different sort of alternative situation. The problem about freedom and regimentation, aside from the matter of defining degrees of the two alternatives, actually is a combination of an alternative proposition and a disjunctive proposition. The full meaning of "It is either Tuesday or Wednesday" would be "It is either Tuesday or Wednesday, but not both." The full meaning of the statement about freedom and regimentation is "We will have either freedom or regimentation, but we will not have both."

We shall call the "either . . . or . . . or both" type of proposition the "weak alternation." It is sometimes called the "inclusive 'or' proposition." We shall call the "either . . . or . . . but not both" proposition the "strong alternation." It is sometimes called the "exclusive 'or' proposition."

## 1. THE WEAK ALTERNATIVE SYLLOGISM

The rules governing the weak alternative syllogism are quite simple for there are only two things which the minor premise may do in a weak alternative proposition. The minor premise may state that one of the alternatives is true, or the minor premise may state that one of the alternatives is false. Our task is therefore quite restricted. Here, then, are the rules governing weak alternation.

Rule 1. If, in the case of a weak alternative proposition, the minor premise affirms one alternative, no conclusion may be stated regarding the other alternative. For example:

> Either Jasper is very intelligent, or he studies
> systematically and well.
> Jasper is very intelligent.
> So Jasper does not study systematically and well.

Such a conclusion would obviously not be justified. Jasper may be intelligent, and he may also study systematically and well. He may be smart enough to do good work without great effort, or he may work hard to overcome some problem not associated with intelligence. We have no way of knowing which from what is given in the premises. Remember, we are always interested in forced conclusions.

Rule 2. If, in the case of a weak alternative proposition, the minor premise denies one alternative, the conclusion must affirm the other. For example:

> Either Jasper is very intelligent, or he studies
> systematically and well.
> Jasper is not very intelligent.
> Therefore Jasper studies systematically and well.

This syllogism is valid. To be sure, the reliability of the conclusion, the soundness of the argument, depends upon our confirmation that the major and minor premises are both true.

In the shorthand of logic we shall use "V" inserted in a proposition to be read as "Either . . . or . . . or both." Further abbreviation may be accomplished by the use of a dash before a term in the minor premise to indicate negation rather than writing out a negative proposition in full. The syllogism about Jasper and his studies would appear in this convenient, abbreviated form:

> Jas. int. V studies.
> — Jasp. int.
> Studies.

## 2. THE DISJUNCTIVE SYLLOGISM

Where the terms of a proposition are mutually exclusive —disjoined—without an "either . . . or . . ." being included either directly or by implication in the proposition, we have what is called a disjunctive proposition. The terms of such a proposition are called "disjuncts." The two rules governing syllogisms involving a disjunctive proposition are very different from those governing alternative syllogisms. They are considered here in turn.

Rule 1. If the minor premise affirms a disjunct in the major premise, the conclusion must deny the other. For example:

> Not both did Taylor vote for the amendment and against the amendment.
> Taylor voted for the amendment.
> Therefore, Taylor did not vote against the amendment.

This is obviously valid. But, it might be noted that economy can be accomplished in time and space and accuracy can be easily assured by writing the syllogism as follows:

> $-$ (T. vote for $\cdot$ against)
> T. voted for.
> $-$ vote against.

The dash represents negation. The parentheses with the dot between the enclosed terms represent the expression "both . . . and. . . ." Thus a dash parenthesis dot parenthesis is to be read "not both . . . and . . ."

Some are sensitive at first to a seemingly awkward expression like "Not both so and so and so and so." But such an expression makes disjunction clear and it is helpful to adjust to the wording.

Rule 2. If the minor premise denies a disjunct in the

major premise, the procedure is invalid, and no conclusion is possible. For example:

> Not both did Taylor vote for the amendment
> and against the amendment.
> Taylor did not vote against the amendment.
> Therefore, . . .

Is a conclusion possible? No. The major premise did not assure that Taylor would actually cast a vote. He may have simply refrained from voting. Or he may have been absent at the time the vote was taken.

Let us examine another illustration.

> It is not the case that Ray is well and has an
> elevation in temperature.
> Ray is not well.
> Therefore, . . .

What can we conclude about Ray's temperature? Nothing at all, for one may be ill and not have an elevation in temperature. Indeed, one may be quite ill and have a reduction in temperature. Symbolized and abbreviated the syllogism would appear thus:

> — (Ray well • elev. temp.)
> — Ray well.
> Therefore, . . .

Or, suppose we reason that we cannot avoid pollution and also have industries careless about waste disposal. That is,

> — (avoid pollution • ind. careless)

If we affirm that we must avoid pollution, then something must be done to correct the carelessness of industries. But, if we deny that we shall avoid pollution, we can say nothing about the industries' efforts to improve the situation by more care, since there are many sources of pollution.

Sometimes an apparently disjunctive proposition appears in which denying a disjunct would seem to yield a conclusion. For example, returning to Congressman Taylor and his voting:

> Not both did Taylor vote for the amendment and refrain from voting for the amendment.
> Taylor did not refrain from voting for the amendment.
> Therefore, Taylor voted for the amendment.

Note carefully the wording of the major premise. This is an alternative disjunctive proposition parading as a disjunctive proposition. By the nature of the situation one cannot both vote for and refrain from voting for a proposed piece of legislation. This, then, is an implied "Either . . . or . . . but not both . . . and . . ." proposition. We now move on to this type of syllogism—the alternative-disjunctive syllogism, or as we shall call it, the "strong alternative syllogism."

### 3. STRONG ALTERNATION

The strong alternative or alternative-disjunctive proposition combines alternation and disjunction. It combines "either . . . or . . ." with "not both . . . and . . ." The two principles governing this type of syllogism can best be stated in one rule, since each principle is the converse of the other. The rule is this:

> If the minor premise affirms either term in a proposition expressing strong alternation, the conclusion must deny the other term; and, if the minor premise denies either term in a proposition expressing strong alternation, the conclusion must affirm the other term.

In the following illustrations the interplay of denying and affirming the terms will illustrate the application of the rule.

> The defendant is either guilty of perjury or not
> guilty of perjury, but not both.
> He is guilty of perjury.
> Therefore, he is not not guilty of perjury.

This is obviously valid. Note, regarding the formal handling of the syllogism, that the minor premise has affirmed the first alternative-disjunct, and the conclusion has denied the second, giving, in this instance, a double negative. By the rules of syntax, a double negative gives an affirmative, one which in this case matches the statement in the minor premise. Or, the syllogism may be restated for further illustrative purposes thus:

> The defendant is either guilty of perjury or not
> guilty of perjury, but not both.
> He is not guilty of perjury.
> Therefore, he is not guilty of perjury.

Note, even though it may seem superfluous, that, in this instance, the minor premise has affirmed the second alternative-disjunct and the conclusion has denied the first. Thus, the syllogism follows the rules governing strong alternation.

Here is another illustration. A man is charged with committing a crime in Dillsboro at 1:00 A.M., November 11, 1975. He succeeds in proving that he was some five hundred miles away from Dillsboro during the entire time from November 9 to November 22, 1975. The alternative-disjunct presented to the jury would go something like this:

> The defendant was either in Dillsboro at the time
> specified for the crime, or he was some five hundred miles away from Dillsboro at the time specified for the crime, but not both.
> The defendant was some five hundred miles away
> from Dillsboro at the time specified for the crime.
> Therefore, the defendant was not in Dillsboro, etc.

If the premises in such a real situation were true, then this syllogism, since it is valid, would yield a reliable conclusion. A jury would act strangely indeed to convict the defendant of the alleged crime.

Suppose, however, witnesses testified to seeing the defendant in Dillsboro a few minutes before or after the time the crime was committed and, therefore, successfully refuted the contention that he was far away. The syllogism in this case would read:

> Either the defendant was in Dillsboro at the time specified for the crime, or he was some five hundred miles away from Dillsboro at the time specified for the crime, but not both.
> The defendant was in Dillsboro at the time specified for the crime.
> Therefore, the defendant was not five hundred miles away.

Not only is the conclusion reliable, having been reached in a valid way, but now the defendant is in difficulty. He may not be guilty of the crime, but he now has the task of supplanting his alibi with some other argument.

A convenient way to place a proposition representing strong alternation in logical shorthand form is to use the symbol "VV" between the terms and to construe its meaning as "Either . . . or . . . but not both." The syllogism above would appear something like this.

> Def. in Dill. VV 500 mi. away.
> Def. in Dill.
> − 500 mi. away.

It is evident from the analysis and illustrations pertaining to the strong alternative syllogism that there is a degree of circularity involved in handling it. But sometimes it is an appropriate and useful element of circularity, as in the illustration we have used.

## 4. DUBIOUS PREMISE RELATIONSHIPS

In the discussion of the categorical syllogism, a section was devoted to the four-term fallacy. One may have a line of argument that is valid because of its form, but unsound or productive of an unreliable conclusion. This may be due to dubious relationships between the terms involved or to premises that are not precisely and definitively stated.

If you say that your favorite college football team will either win or lose, you have ignored the reality of the sport that there is a third alternative, a tie. If someone owes you a thousand dollars, and payment depends upon proceeds from a ten thousand dollar suit he has entered in court, you may reason, "Either he will win or lose, but not both, and so my receipt of payment is at stake." Your spirits fall when you learn he did not win his claim of ten thousand dollars. But, it is possible they may soar again when it develops he was awarded seventy-five hundred dollars, more than enough to cover his debt to you.

If a friend tells you that he is applying for a foundation grant and is struggling to meet a deadline of October 1, you conclude, "Either Boggs will get his application in on time and have it duly considered or he will not, but not both." You encounter him mailing his application and conspectus barely in time and congratulate him upon the award he is about to receive. The congratulations may be premature, for you are not sure that the foundation's reaction to the proposal he has made will be favorable. You cannot even be sure the foundation will consider his application, for the announcement of grants merely eliminated from consideration all tardy applications. On the other hand, if you learn that the deadline passed before Boggs completed the preparation of his application, you will be justified in commiserating with him, for you will conclude properly that he will receive neither consideration nor the grant.

## Exercises: Chapter 10

Examine the following syllogisms, putting them in logical shorthand form, and comment upon their validity and reliability.

1. A book may be appreciated for its useful content, or for its style.
   *The Physics of the Atom* has useful content.
   Therefore its style is not to be appreciated.

2. "I appreciate this book and I only appreciate a book for its useful content or for its style. I do not like its style, however."
   "Then it must have content useful to you."

3. Frazzell is either a representative or a senator.
   He is a representative.
   Therefore he is not a senator.

4. Frazzell is either a representative or a senator.
   He is not a senator.
   Therefore Frazzell is a representative.

5. "Either Barbara or Totsie will be joining me for dinner, and I see here's Barbara."
   "Well, I suppose Totsie will not be joining you."

6. "Either Spadly will do a critical book review for this course, or he will flunk."
   "I happen to know he's on his way with his review, so I'm relieved that he will pass."

7. "We must maintain detente with Russia, or world tensions will surely increase; and we are going to maintain that detente."

"Well, I'm certainly happy with the notion that world tensions are not going to increase."

8. Nixon must either meet the terms of the committee and deliver the subpoenaed tapes, or the Republicans will lose more and more elections.
   Nixon does not meet the terms of the committee.
   Therefore the Republicans will lose more and more elections.

9. Surely, one will not embezzle money and report it to the IRS on his income tax form.
   Spelkes has embezzled some money.
   Therefore he will report it, as regulations imply he must.

10. To be able to retire comfortably these days, one must either have been lucky enough to inherit money or be wise in budgeting and investments.
    Ray says he is going to retire comfortably, and he has not inherited any money at all.
    So Ray must have been wise in budgeting and investment.

11. It is either winter, spring, summer, or fall.
    It is winter.
    Therefore it is neither spring summer nor fall.

12. It is either winter, spring, summer, or fall.
    It is not winter.
    Therefore it is either spring, summer, or fall.

13. Either Nixon knew nothing about Watergate, which would indicate he is not alert to events, or he disdains moral and legal responsibility. No evidence has been adduced to indicate he knew anything about Watergate.
    Therefore Nixon does not disdain moral and legal responsibility.

14. Dick Tuck was either a gross parader of practical jokes
    or a political idealist.
    He is by no means a political idealist.
    So he stands as a gross practical joker.
15. Dick Tuck was either a gross practical joker, or he
    was a political idealist.
    He was certainly a gross practical joker.
    So he was by no means a political idealist.

### Comments on Exercises for Chapter 10

1.                              Cont. V style.
                                Cont.
                                — style.

Invalid. The minor premise affirms one alternative in a
major premise that represents weak or simple alternation.
Clearly, a book may be appreciated either for its useful
content or for its style or for both.

2.                              Cont. V style.
                                — style.
                                Cont.

Valid. If one appreciates a book, the appreciation may
be utilitarian or esthetic or both. If, in this case the reader
is limited to these possibilities, and he appreciates the
book but denies he likes its style, then, obviously, he likes
its useful contents.

3.                              Rep. VV Sen.
                                Rep.
                                — Sen.

Valid, for the major premise is strong alternation by the
categories represented, in that the terms are a case of combining alternation and disjunction. "Frazzell is either a
representative or a senator, but not both."

4.                     Rep. VV Sen.
                               — Sen.
                               Rep.

Valid. The minor premise denies one of the alternative-disjunctive terms, forcing the affirmation of the other.

5. Invalid. An alternative is affirmed in simple alternation. The major premise does not rule out the enjoyment of the company of both friends.
6. Invalid. An alternative is affirmed in simple alternation. The major premise does not assure that handing in a critical review will result in passing the course. It only asserts that failing to do the assignment will result in failure in the course.
7. Invalid. An alternative is affirmed in simple alternation.
8. Valid. An alternative is denied.

9.                     — (embezzle • rep.)
                             Embezzle.
                             Report.

Invalid. This is a case of simple disjunction. One disjunct has been affirmed in the minor premise, and, therefore, the conclusion must deny and not affirm, as it has done, the other.

10. Valid. Weak alternation, with the minor premise denying one alternative and the conclusion affirming the other.
11. Valid. Strong alternation.
12. Valid. Strong alternation.
13. Invalid, on two counts. The minor premise affirms an alternative in simple alternation and, in this case, does so by committing the fallacy of appeal to ignorance.
14. Valid. Weak alternation.
15. Invalid. Dick Tuck may have been both.

# Chapter 11

# The Dilemma

"I've dawdled too much this quarter. Now, if I spend my time on physics my grades in general will be low, and if I spend time on all my courses, I risk flunking physics. What a dilemma!"

"Nixon's got a problem. If he turns over all his tapes, by his own admission they may be construed as showing him guilty of wrongdoing. If he refuses to turn them over, he is sure to be judged as guilty and lose support. He's in a dilemma."

"If I invest in insurance policies, inflation will eat up their value later. But, if I do not take out insurance, I will leave my family unprotected."

"If we continue to rent, monthly checks for rent will strain our budget to the breaking point. If we buy a house, high interest rates will strain our budget to the breaking point."

## 1. The Three Types of Dilemma

Dilemma means two (from the Greek *di*) assumptions (from the Greek *lemma*). The term "assumption" reminds us that hypothetical propositions are involved. As the illustrations show, a dilemma involves two hypothetical propositions, or assumptions. Before we face again some personal dilemma of our own, let us calmly study the three forms of the dilemma, conventionally spoken of as:

1. The Simple Constructive Dilemma
2. The Complex Constructive Dilemma
3. The Destructive Dilemma, which is always complex

The constructive dilemma is not called constructive because it is pleasant to contemplate, although some dilemmas—whether to go to the movie or the concert, whether to vacation at the beach or in the mountains, whether to have pecan or chocolate pie—present pleasant alternatives. The distinction between the constructive and destructive forms of the dilemma is, rather, that the constructive is affirmatively stated along the lines of the syllogism, while the destructive involves negatives in the minor premise.

The Simple Constructive Dilemma has the following form:

> If A is B, C is D; and if E is F, C is D.
> Either A is B, or E is F.
> Therefore, C is D.

All forms of the dilemma combine two conditional (or hypothetical) statements in the major premise and an alternative-disjunct in the minor premise. In the Simple Constructive Dilemma above the antecedents in each hypothetical proposition are different (If A is B and if E is F) while the consequents are the same (therefore C is D), hence "simple." The terms of the minor premise are affirmative, hence "constructive." Examine the plight of the young couple, mentioned earlier, contemplating rent versus house purchase:

> If we rent, our budget will be strained;
>   if we buy, our budget will be strained.
> We must rent or buy.
> Therefore, our budget will be strained.

The Complex Constructive Dilemma has the following form:

> If A is B, C is D; and if E is F, G is H.
> Either A is B or E is F.
> Therefore either C is D or G is H.

Consider the person concerned about insurance matters:

> If I insure, inflation will devalue the insurance, and if I
>   do not insure, my family will be unprotected.
> I must either insure or not insure.
> Therefore either inflation will devalue the insurance or
>   my family will be unprotected.

In this illustration, there are involved four different terms linked in the hypothetical and alternative-disjunctive propositions, and the terms of the minor premise are affirmative, hence "complex constructive." (Note that the "not insure" in the minor premise is an affirmation of the "not insure" in the second conditional of the major premise.)

The Destructive Dilemma has the following form:

> If A is B, C is D; and if E is F, G is H.
> Either C is not D, or G is not H.
> Therefore, either A is not B, or E is not F.

Neither of the introductory illustrations represents this type of dilemma, but the nineteenth century Archbishop Whateley offered one we may use:

If a man is wise, he does not mock the Scriptures in jest;
and if a man is good, he does not mock the Scriptures
seriously.
This man mocks the Scriptures either in jest or seriously.
Thus, this man is either not wise, or he is not good.

## 2. MEETING DILEMMATIC ARGUMENTS

*Testing for Validity.*

If in the statement of a dilemmatic syllogism either of
the rules governing the hypothetical or the alternative-disjunctive syllogism is broken, then the dilemma is not a
true one and may be dismissed. Unfortunately, such a situation is rarely encountered, for one facing a real life situation seems automatically to affirm the antecedent in the
hypothetical proposition (s) and follow through with the
alternative. But, a casual examination of the accuracy of
the structure will do no harm. First, then, check the structure for validity in form.

*Seizing a Horn.*

Some writers use the term "Breaking a Horn," and the
expression is appropriate if, upon seizing a horn, one is
able to break it or wrestle down the figurative charging
bull. But, only the outcome of events can show whether the
horn was successfully broken. Therefore, "seizing a horn"
seems a more appropriate label. The initial step in this
procedure is deciding which horn to seize. Examine the
illustration given for the simple constructive dilemma:

Rent $\supset$ budget strained; buy $\supset$ budget strained.
Rent VV buy.
Therefore budget strained.

Notice that the minor premise has been expressed as

strong alternation, for it is hardly likely a couple in budgetary straits would both rent and buy.

Obviously, a young couple should spend some time systematically examining the want ads, discussing their problem with responsible real estate companies, and perhaps even discussing budgetary matters with a marriage counseling service. The couple may find an apartment within their means, rent it, and thus seize (and break) the first horn. Or, the couple may discover a house whose cost is within their means or whose plan of financing will not strain their budget. In this case, the second horn is seized and broken.

Seizing the horn of some complex constructive dilemmas can be a bit more dubious as to results. Consider the person with the insurance problem:

> Insure ⊃ inflation devalue, and not insure ⊃ family unprotected.
> Insure VV not insure.
> Inflation devalue VV family unprotected.

The person may find a combination of insurance investment plans that will cover the family and yet hedge against inflation. In which case, the first horn has been seized. Of course, only future developments will reveal whether the horn broke or not. Similarly, if the person does not insure, but invests in stocks, bonds, or what not, the second horn will be seized, and, again, success or failure will be known only in the future.

*Escaping Between the Horns.*

Often, fortunately, one stating a dilemma commits the black-or-white fallacy. That is, he states only two alternatives when, in fact, there are others. An Athenian mother is reported to have counseled her son not to enter public service: "If, in public service, you speak unjustly, the gods will hate you; and, my son, if you speak justly, men will hate you!" This doting mother ignored the possibility that there are important posts in public service which do not require either policy making or commentary upon policy.

A devout minister so strongly wanted his son to follow in his footsteps that he seemed inclined not to finance the young man's college education if he chose another profession. The young man was fond of and competent in music, and so was his fiancée. Moreover, his fiancée did not relish being a minister's wife. The young man resolved the problem by preparing for a career in arranging and publishing music, in which a considerable portion of his time could be devoted to sacred music. All three parties to this problem were satisfied with the decision. The sharp horns of a dilemma had been eluded.

### Establishing a Counter Dilemma

Since dilemmas do not always reveal all of the aspects of the situation or situations they involve, it is often possible to pose a counter dilemma. Since this is essentially a mechanical procedure, the resultant dilemma may simply be more psychologically satisfying than the original dilemma. The counter dilemma is established by *exchanging* the *places* of the *consequents* in the major premise and *negating* them.

For example, suppose the Athenian lad had said to his mother: "If I speak justly, the gods will *not* hate me and if I speak unjustly, men will *not* hate me" he would have posed a counter dilemma. He has interchanged the consequents and negated each of them. To be sure, he still faces the prospect of someone disapproving of him, but he is at least looking on the bright side of things.

Similarly, if the young man whose father was a minister

had said, "If I prepare for the ministry, my father will support me; and if I choose another profession, Meg will marry me," he would have posed a counter dilemma. Again, the choice is not without its unfortunate facets, but the young man has made one strike for happiness for someone or two in the threesome involved.

## A Reminder

A necessary condition for clear thinking is calm self-confidence, and a constructive, inquiring mindset. We have a store of information about analysis we have to keep in mind as we look at advertisements, listen to news commentators, attend political rallies, or sit in a class or pew. We have some three dozen material and linguisitic fallacies to sort out. We have to frame various types of syllogisms from allegedly logical arguments. An attitude of confidence and thoughtfulness is particularly helpful when one faces a dilemma.

Suppose a middle-aged man of fairly sedentary habits drives past a stream on a cold morning and sees a child on the other side of the river struggling in the water. He may wring his hands helplessly, saying to himself, "If I try to swim over, I will surely go into shock from the chilly water. If I don't plunge in and do what I can, I will have nightmares the rest of my life."

There is no use entering a counter dilemma at this point. Certainly a counter dilemma doesn't seem a satisfactory solution, for a counter dilemma would go thus: "If I try to swim over I will not have nightmares the rest of my life, and if I don't plunge in I will not go into shock from the chilly water." Seizing a horn appears to be an unsatisfactory solution. A plunge may, indeed, produce severe shock, and not plunging in the river may, indeed, subject him to recurring nightmares. Why does he not busy himself im-

mediately by calling for help from the other side, flagging
down a passing car with some stalwart young man or
woman in it, or taking a more modest risk than plunging
in, by floating out on his spare tire or that empty plastic
container in his trunk compartment?

Fortunately, such extreme dilemmas as this, requiring
split second decisions, come rarely. But, envisioning their
possibility helps us prepare for them; and, for dilemmas
not requiring immediate action, by studying their pro-
perties beforehand, we can be more effectively deliberative
when they occur.

### EXERCISES: CHAPTER 11

Identify the following as to the nature of the dilemma,
whether Simple Constructive, Complex Constructive, etc.,
and examine the dilemma as to the way or ways it might
be handled. Identify your choice as to the preferred way.

1. If income taxes are reduced, more spendable income
   will increase inflation. If income taxes are not reduced,
   the government will continue to spend, thus increasing
   inflation.
   Taxes either will or will not be reduced. Therefore,
   continuing inflation is inevitable.

2. If we aid underdeveloped countries, they become increasingly dependent upon us. If we decline to aid
   them, we lose their friendship and they turn to somewhat hostile countries.
   Either we extend aid to underdeveloped countries, or
   we refrain from doing so. Therefore, we face their becoming dependent or allied with hostile countries.

3. A professor reasons: "If a student is interested in
   learning, I need make no effort to motivate him. If he
   lacks interest in learning, my efforts to motivate him
   will be fruitless. Students are either interested in or

lack interest in learning. So, I need make no effort at motivating them."

4. Pragmatists have been known to criticize syllogistic reasoning in the following manner: "For a syllogism to be valid, it must be circular in its argument, bringing out no new insight, and is, therefore, without value. If a syllogism is invalid, it is clearly without value. A syllogism must be either valid or invalid. Therefore, a syllogism is without value."

5. The slogan "Love It or Leave It" seems to imply the following line of reasoning. "If you believe in the capitalistic system, you should stop criticizing it. If you do not believe in it, then you should move to Russia. Either you believe in the capitalistic system, or you do not; therefore, either you should cease being critical, or move to Russia."

6. If the dean were a prudent man, he would not say truthfully that he has refused a tenured faculty appointment. If he were fully honest, he would not say falsely that he has refused a tenured faculty appointment. The dean has said that he has refused such an appointment; therefore, he is either imprudent or not fully honest.

## COMMENTS ON EXERCISES FOR CHAPTER 11

Identifying the form or nature of a dilemma is of less practical value than the exercise of thinking through the various implications of the terms of the dilemma. But, identifying its form may be of some help by allowing the immediate elimination of some ways of meeting the dilemma. The first exercise in this series is a case in point.

1. A simple constructive dilemma.

Posing a counter dilemma for a simple constructive dilemma is an exercise in futility. In the present case the counter dilemma would read, "If income taxes are not reduced, inflation will not increase; and if income taxes are reduced, inflation will not increase." We have followed the proper procedure in stating a counter dilemma. We have exchanged the positions of the consequents and negated them. But, since the consequents of the dilemma and the counter dilemma are identical, all we have done is to deny the truth of the hypothetical propositions which constitute the dilemma. And, if we can deny the truth of each, or of either, we do not have a real dilemma.

There is no escape between the horns of this dilemma for it is clearly an "either . . . or . . . but not both "situation. Income taxes will either be reduced or not reduced.

Thus we are forced to consider seizing a horn. If congress reduces taxes, such a move might be accompanied by other measures to control inflation, such as a persuasive campaign to get the public to invest tax savings only in goods and services, so that inflation would not be increased. Price and wage controls might be written into law, or government expenditures in areas which contribute to inflation might be curbed. If either or all of these combined serve to control inflation, then the first horn would have been broken.

If income taxes are left intact, various branches of government might collaborate in reducing expenditures in appropriate areas to control inflation or investing receipts in programs that would modify the tendency to inflation. If such should be effective, the second horn would have been broken.

These suggestions do not by any means exhaust the possibilities for attempting to meet the dilemma but they illustrate procedures one would follow in examining it.

2. A complex constructive dilemma.

There seems to be no escape between the horns of this dilemma. Either we aid underdeveloped countries or we decline to aid them. Aiding them only a little would still be aiding them.

There may be some comfort, but it will be small for sensitive persons, in establishing a counter dilemma: "If we decline to aid underdeveloped countries, they will not become increasingly dependent upon us; and if we aid them, they will not become less friendly and turn to hostile countries." One of the difficulties with this procedure is that aiding countries has not always assured their continuing friendship with us.

Seizing a horn, then, seems to be a possible alternative. Aid the underdeveloped countries, but not so heavily that they become dependent, and aid them in ways that will enable them to be increasingly self-sufficient.

If the second horn is seized and aid is declined, it probably could be broken only if we were very persuasive that we were in a position that made it impossible to extend aid, or if we could persuade them that it would not be at all in their interest to turn to hostile countries for friendship and aid.

In many dilemmas such as this one, it is virtually impossible to avoid subjective elements in deciding which horn one would prefer to seize. It is very likely that one-world advocates would seize the first horn, and that those inclined to isolationism would seize the second.

3. A simple constructive dilemma.

Even though there are negatives in certain terms of

this dilemma, it is simple constructive in form, and not destructive, because of the positioning of the negatives.

Escaping between the horns of a dilemma requires an alternative to the choices presented. In this case, there may be students who are neither interested nor disinterested in study, and yet are not uninterested in study. With these students, the professor should try motivation, although one may suspect that the dilemma he presents is a rationalization. Immanuel Kant reported his attitude toward students something like this: "I devote attention to the average student. The competent student does not need my help. The poor student will not profit by it anyway." But, some resist study, and others are very interested in learning. With these, the Kantian escape route is not open.

A counter dilemma has possibilities, if the professor is not seeking to escape responsibility. "If a student is not interested in learning, I should make a great effort to motivate him. If a student is interested in learning, my efforts at further motivation should be very fruitful." The counter dilemma and the possibility of seizing a horn are very much alike in this instance.

4. A simple constructive dilemma.

One may seize the first horn of the dilemma by denying that circular arguments are always without value. The use of the Pythagorean theorem regarding right angle triangles is a good illustration. One assumes the validity, and circularity, of this syllogism: "All right angle triangles have the quality that the square of the hypotenuse is equal to the sum of the squares of the other two sides. This triangle (of which I have stepped off two sides, the third side being an imaginary line across a lake) is a right angle triangle. Therefore, since the square of the hypotenuse (which is the imaginary line across the lake) equals the sum of the squares of the sides I have stepped off, I can now determine the width of the lake without rowboat and rope."

Seizing the second horn of the dilemma is somewhat, but not entirely, fatuous. If a syllogism is invalid, it may not be entirely without value; for example, it may reveal a fruitless line of reasoning which can be eliminated so that we may follow another.

Escape between the horns or entering a counter dilemma does not appear to work with this dilemma.

5.  A complex constructive dilemma.

One might well ask the sloganeer, "Do you really wish that those who are critical of the capitalistic system would defect to Russia, thus bearing witness to the unbearability of our system? Would you not rather consider their criticisms, making adjustments if they are valid and refuting them if they are not?" This question prompts one to seek an escape between the horns. "I do not believe in capitalism, believe in the sense that I am not fully committed to capitalism as currently practiced, but I do not disbelieve so strongly that I wish to be a Russian-style Communist. I am open to being convinced, so I shall stay."

In this case a counter dilemma has more merit than first meets the eye. "If I do not believe in the capitalistic system, I should not move to Russia, but remain here and work for radical revision of the system. If I do believe in the capitalistic system, I should stop criticizing it, but continually be examining it with a view to its improvement."

Seizing a horn of this dilemma would require more mental dexterity to avoid being gored than either of the approaches just suggested.

6.  A complex constructive dilemma.

A counter dilemma in this situation would be as unbefitting a dean as would seizing the second horn. Placing the antecedent of the second hypothetical proposition with the consequent of the first would be internally inconsistent. And the next juxtaposition would yield this: "If the dean were a prudent man, he would say falsely that he has refused a tenured faculty appointment."

In the actual situation, the dean could not escape between the horns of the dilemma by saying nothing. For, it so happened that he had been jockeyed into answering a direct question during a warm discussion with his faculty over the question of tenure policies. To complete the sad, real life story, he seized the first horn, but, in due course, was proved to be imprudent and, also, improvident as regards his family. During a sweeping change in administration personnel, he found himself out of the deanship with no faculty position to resort to.

# Chapter 12

# Direct Inference

Reading between the lines is a rather common practice. It is, of course, a psychological rather than a logical procedure. Related to this practice is that of adding more to a proposition than a speaker or writer intended the proposition to convey. One way in which this happens is for one to infer from an affirmative proposition that a negative based upon it always conveys information, or to infer from a negative proposition that an affirmative proposition based upon it must also convey information.

Suppose one says, "All communists believe in public housing," and a hearer infers, "Then, those who are not communists do not believe in public housing," the hearer has read into the proposition more than has been specifically stated. Or, if the hearer infers, "Therefore, all who believe in public housing are communists," he has again read more into the proposition than its wording justifies.

One may hear a very brief news note which reports, "Some of the oil producing nations will not be represented at the conference on the economics of transportation." It would be unwarranted to conclude, "I have just learned from the news that some of the oil producing companies will have representatives at the conference on the economics of transportation."

In several of the preceding chapters we have dealt with "mediate" inference, or inference using more than one proposition, with a middle or mediating term to guide us to a possible conclusion or assist us in determining that no conclusion is possible. From the paragraphs introducing this chapter, we see that it is important to examine what happens when we deduce information from a single proposition. Without proceeding with illustrations of the various ways in which information may be deduced from single propositions, and without discussing the forms of handling single propositions that will not yield further valid information, let us take up in order the various forms that propositions take and discuss what may and may not be done in shifting parts of them about. Recall that the classification of propositions used here is presented in Chapter 7.

### 1. THE A-FORM PROPOSITION, OR THE UNIVERSAL AFFIRMATIVE

The statement of a clear, understandable, universal affirmative proposition, especially one accepted as true, conveys more information than its original form delivers. Let us examine, for example, what appears to be a true universal proposition that:

All migrant workers depend upon seasonal employment. If we shift this to the E-form, or universal negative, retaining the same subject and predicate: "No migrant workers are dependent upon seasonal employment," we have stated a false proposition, assuming, to repeat, that the initial proposition is true. Thus, the truth of an A-form (universal affirmative) proposition renders its E-form false. This can be conveniently symbolized by an arrow pointing horizontally to the right from an A-form proposition to its E-form with the arrow labeled "F" for false, thus:

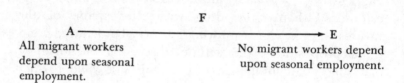

$$F$$

A ————————————————————————————→ E

All migrant workers                        No migrant workers depend
depend upon seasonal                   upon seasonal employment.
employment.

We may state an I-form (particular affirmative) proposition based upon the original statement and gain at least partial truth: "Some migrant workers depend upon seasonal employment." This statement does not cover the entire class of migrant workers, but if "All migrant workers depend upon seasonal employment" is true, so is the proposition "Some migrant workers depend upon seasonal employment." We can symbolize this by having an arrow point vertically from the A-form proposition to its I-form, with the arrow labeled "T" to indicate that the truth of an A-form proposition ("All . . . are . . .") implies the truth of an I-form proposition ("Some . . . are . . .") using the same subject and predicate.

All migrant workers depend upon seasonal employment.

A

T

Some migrant workers depend upon seasonal employment.

I

We now have two lines of the eight lines which form the square of opposition, a figure which will prove very convenient for prompt recognition of the relation of various propositional forms.

Just as the truth of an A-form proposition implies the falsity of its E-form proposition, so too does the A-form proposition imply the falsity of its O-form proposition.

Obviously if "All migrant workers depend upon seasonal employment" is true then it is false that "Some migrant workers do not depend upon seasonal employment." Let us represent this by having an arrow point diagonally down to the right from A to O, labeled F to show falsity is implied.

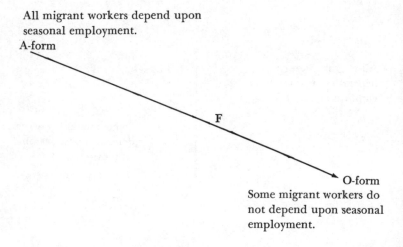

All migrant workers depend upon
seasonal employment.
A-form

F

O-form
Some migrant workers do
not depend upon seasonal
employment.

## 2. The E-form Proposition, or the Universal Negative

Beginning now with the E-form proposition, and leaving migrant workers for a time, accept the proposition "No backpackers litter trails." If this is true, then it is false that "All backpackers litter trails," and it is also false that "Some backpackers litter trails." Furthermore, if the E-form proposition "No backpackers litter trails" is true, then the O-form proposition based upon its subject and predicate terms "Some backpackers do not litter trails" is also true. We may now speed up the process of constructing the square of opposition by adding an arrowhead pointing toward A (on the arrow bearing an "F" for false already pointing from A to E), an arrow labeled "T" for true pointing from E directly down toward O, and an arrow labeled "F" for false pointing diagonally down to the left from E to I.

All backpackers
litter trails.

No backpackers
litter trails.

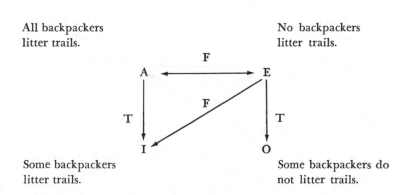

Some backpackers
litter trails.

Some backpackers do
not litter trails.

If one wishes to establish that the E-form proposition "No backpackers litter trails" is false, it is only necessary to find one trail-littering backpacker. An arrowhead pointing from I to E and labeled "F" for false would represent this unhappy discovery. Similarly, to establish that the A-form proposition, "All backpackers litter trails," is false we would only have to find a few very careful, considerate backpackers—or even one. An arrowhead, then, may be pointed from O to A and labeled F to represent this situation.

All backpackers
litter trails.

No backpackers
litter trails.

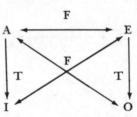

Some backpackers
litter trails.

Some backpackers do
not litter trails.

A word of caution is appropriate here. Universal propositions are often difficult or impossible to defend as true or refute as false. They can be demonstrated true or false in limited, controlled situations. Here is an example of the difficulty of proving an E-proposition. An instructor was describing to a class how the use of the term "radical" has changed through the years. In early usage, "radical" meant "linked with the center of something", in the sense of being well rooted. In the course of time, "radical" was applied to idealists, political leftists, and others who seemed to have become rootless. Then, at about the middle of the twentieth century, users of the word used it as an adjective to describe rightist groups, so that phrases like "radical right" appeared in our language. A student protested, " 'Radical' is never used in that way, and I can prove it." Not wishing to embarrass the student, the instructor passed over the remark but talked with the student after class, saying, "One should be very careful about statements such as the one you made about the phrase 'radical right.' How could you prove that the combination of words is *never* used? You handed me a decided advantage, but I did not wish to pursue it. You see, it would be nearly impossible to prove that 'radical' is *never* used to modify 'right'. You and I would have to read every recent newspaper and periodical in our library, and listen to every radio and television broadcast of news and panel discussions of the last couple of decades. Now it so happens that I have just read an article in a current magazine describing a particular radio station as being controlled by the 'radical right.' All we have to do is to go to the library for me to show it to you, and your statement will be proved false."

In a controlled or limited situation, of course, one can sometimes establish a universal negative proposition. If I were to say, "None of the books in my personal library bear nameplates," a little time spent checking my books for nameplates would determine whether or not the proposition is true.

### 3. THE I-FORM PROPOSITION, OR THE PARTICULAR AFFIRMATIVE; AND THE O-FORM PROPOSITION, OR THE PARTICULAR NEGATIVE.

The relation of I-form and O-form propositions to A-form and E-form propositions and to each other remains to be considered. From the truth of an I-form proposition, it can be correctly inferred that its E-form expression is false. However, the truth of an I-form proposition tells us nothing about either its A-form or its O-form. The truth of an O-form proposition tells us that its A-form is false but does not determine the truth or falseness of either its I-form or its E-form.

If one infers from the proposition "Some beer drinkers are litterbugs" that "All beer drinkers are litterbugs," he is generalizing much too broadly. While it appears to be true that a discouragingly large number of beer drinkers are litterbugs, most of us know a few beer drinkers who scrupulously follow the exhortation which appears on some beer can tops, "Please don't litter. Dispose of properly." To extend a "Some . . . are . . ." statement into an "All . . . are . . ." statement may be a case of hasty generalization or, in more formal logical wording, a commission of the fallacy of converse accident. It is certainly an incorrect handling of direct or immediate inference.

One may not properly infer from the truth of an O-form proposition the truth of its E-form. That is, "Some men do not enjoy opera" may not be construed as implying that "No men enjoy opera." From comic strips like "Bringing Up Father" (also known simply as "Maggie and Jiggs") and from various jokes about the foibles of men in regard to culture, it may be observed that opera lacks completely widespread appeal among men. But, if we concede the truth of the proposition "Some men do not enjoy opera," we do not necessarily also concede that "No men enjoy opera." Too many men either enjoy opera or have male friends who do, to accept such a universal negative proposition.

There may now be added to our developing square of opposition two more arrows, one pointing vertically from I to A, and one pointing vertically from O to E. These two arrows are labeled "D" for doubtful, indicating that the truth of an I-form proposition does not tell us whether its A-form is true, and that the truth of an O-form proposition does not tell us whether its E-form is true.

All men enjoy opera.

No men enjoy opera.

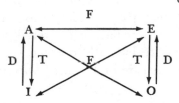

Some men enjoy opera.

Some men do not enjoy opera.

What does the truth of an I-form proposition reveal about its O-form counterpart? What does the truth of an O-form proposition tell us about its I-form counterpart? Nothing whatever. Even so, inferring "Some . . . are not . . ." from "Some . . . are . . ." and inferring "Some . . . are . . ." from "Some . . . are not . . ." is a fairly widespread tendency.

"Some poets are inclined to be gay" seems to be true whether "gay" is defined in its early meaning of merry, its later meaning of indulgent, or its more recent meaning of inclined to romantic attachment to members of one's own sex. This proposition does not tell us, however, that "Some poets are *not* inclined to be gay." We may know from acquaintance that some poets are morbid, some are ascetic, and some are rigidly heterosexual. That is, we may know from observation that they are not gay, but we cannot properly derive this data from the original expression "Some poets are inclined to be gay" itself.

"Some ministers of the gospel are not basically domineering types" may psychologically hint that the one who states the proposition has encountered some ministers of the gospel who are basically domineering types. But, the latter proposition cannot be justifiably derived from the original.

We now can complete our square of opposition by adding a single double-tipped arrow pointing from I to O and from O to I and labeling it "D" for doubtful.

The square of opposition is now complete, and it is simple to use, after a little practice. Given two to four propositions that are related through the subject-verb sequence, simply place the first proposition asserted as true on its proper corner of the diagram, a procedure which can be imagined and not necessarily written out. The

All jurists aim at
impartiality.

No jurists aim at
impartiality.

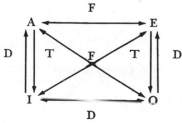

Some jurists aim
at impartiality.

Some jurists do not
aim at impartiality

square then readily reveals whether the other proposition (s) is (are) true, false, or in doubt.

For those who may wish to pursue the use of the square of opposition further, the following technical labels are presented.

If a student will examine the square, either using propositions given in earlier figures as illustrations or supplying his own, he can note that the following important principles hold true:

1. Contradictory propositions cannot both be true, and they cannot both be false.

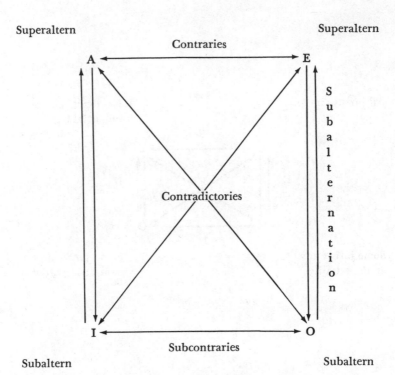

2. Contrary propositions cannot both be true, but they can both be false.
3. Subcontrary propositions can both be true, but they cannot both be false.
4. If a universal proposition is true, its subaltern is also true.
5. If a particular proposition is true, its superaltern is doubtful in the sense that it is undetermined.
6. If a universal proposition is false, its subaltern is doubtful in the sense of being undetermined.
7. If a particular proposition is false, its superaltern is also false.

The following table reviews what has been presented in some detail about what may or may not be immediately inferred given the *truth* of an A-form, E-form, I-form or O-form proposition. There has been added what may or may not be determined from A-form, E-form, I-form, or O-form propositions which are *false*.

| | True | False | Undetermined |
|---|---|---|---|
| I. Given as True | | | |
| A | I | E,O | |
| E | O | A,I | |
| I | | E | A,O |
| O | | A | E,I |
| II. Given as False | | | |
| A | O | | E,I |
| E | I | | A,O |
| I | E,O | A | |
| O | A,I | E | |

Part I of the table has been illustrated in some detail in the preceding discussion. The following, then, are brief illustrations of Part II of the table.

If we are told that the statement "All apples are red" is false, then all we can infer is that "Some apples are not red" is true. The falsity of the given proposition does not justify our stating either that "All apples are not red" or "Some apples are red."

All that is necessary to render an E-proposition as false is to contradict it. And its contradictory is an I-proposition. Thus, if we are told that "No apples are red" is false, then we can infer only that "Some apples are red" is true. We cannot go so far as to say that "All apples are red" or even that "Some apples are not red."

If we know that "Some apples are red" is false, then "No apples are red" is true, and, therefore, "Some apples are not red" is also true. Each of the latter being true then it is also necessarily false that "All apples are red."

If "Some apples are not red" is false, then "All apples (and also, therefore, some apples) are red" is true. "No apples are red," it follows, must be false.

### 4. CONVERSION, OBVERSION, CONTRAPOSITION, AND THE USE OF THE SQUARE OF OPPOSITION*

The converse of a proposition, the obverse of a proposition, and the contraposition of a proposition cannot be placed on the square. This seeming limitation to the use of the square of opposition is actually a feature of some value. What this means is that such propositions can be spotted immediately as not appropriate to the square, and they therefore must be examined individually.

Suppose we say, "All alligators are a protected species." The converse form, "All protected species are alligators," cannot be placed on the square of opposition. We should, by now, recognize the latter proposition as a case of erroneous conversion. A properly converted form would read, "Some protected species are alligators."

Or suppose we say, "All alligators are a protected species" and then say, "No alligators are unprotected as a species." The latter proposition does not fit onto the square of opposition. But, we should be able to tell at a glance that the second proposition is true (if the original is true) because the original proposition has been obverted correctly.

Contraposition has not been discussed before and is not terribly important. Contraposition of propositions is really more an amusing game than it is a serious logical technique. It is also sometimes used for rhetorical effect. So, for relaxation, let us play the game for a bit.

Contraposition is simply the process of reversing the subject and the predicate of a proposition (or pivoting the

---

*A review of conversion and obversion in Chapter 1, Sections 6 and 7 is recommended at this point.

proposition at its verb) and then negating each. The following is an illustration. The contraposition of the proposition "All politicians are somewhat extroverted" is "All who are not somewhat extroverted are nonpoliticians." Or to use a briefer and perhaps clearer illustration, the contrapositive of "All mammals are warmblooded" is "All non-warmblooded animals are non-mammals."

The step-by-step procedure for forming the contrapositive goes like this. First, one states a proposition, then obverts the proposition, then converts the obverted form, and then obverts the converted obverse. To illustrate this procedure, let us repeat our simple, acceptable proposition about mammals and warmbloodedness.

| Original: | 1. All mammals are warmblooded. |
| Obverse of 1: | 2. No mammals are not warmblooded. |
| Converse of 2: | 3. No non-warmblooded animals are mammals. |
| Obverse of 3: | 4. All non-warmblooded animals are non-mammals. |

Proposition number 4 is the contrapositive of the original proposition, number 1.

It is interesting that an A-form proposition and its contradictory, its O-form proposition, can be contraposed, but that an E-form proposition and its I-form proposition cannot. Having just contraposed an A-form proposition, let us now contrapose an O-form proposition.

| Original: | 1. Some canine corps dogs are not retrainable. |
| Obverse of 1: | 2. Some canine corps dogs are non-retrainable. |
| Converse of 2: | 3. Some non-retrainable dogs are canine corps dogs. |
| Obverse of 3: | 4. Some non-retrainable dogs are not non-canine corps dogs. |

That worked out smoothly, but let us now try to contra-pose an E-form proposition.

Original:        1.  No men are fifty-feet tall.
Obverse of 1:    2.  All men are non-fifty-feet tall.

We obviously cannot convert this proposition to read "All non-fifty-foot tall things are men." We must be content, then, with conversion by limitation, with the final step resulting not in full contraposition, but in contraposition by limitation:

Converse of 2 above:   3.  Some non-fifty-foot tall things
                           are men.
Obverse of 3:          4.  Some non-fifty-foot tall things are
                           not non-men.

Another term for this is "partial contraposition."

Those who have read the section in the appendix dealing with the "existential particular" would look at this another way. The original proposition "No men are fifty-feet tall" does not declare whether the category of things "fifty-feet tall" is actually occupied. Let the proposition read "No men are 1,000,000 feet tall" and it may be clear that we are not declaring the category "1,000,000 feet tall" occupied. The final statement of partial contraposition, by the rule concerning the existential particular, implies that it is occupied. This is a reason for being careful with I-form propositions and with contraposition by limitation. Both involve an existential assumption.

Back to our less abstruse, practical type of analysis, consider the proposition we would accept as true, "No heavy-weight boxers are flabby." If we were to contrapose this directly—that is, reverse subject and predicate and negate each in turn—we would have, "No flabby persons are non-heavyweight boxers." There are, we are quite sure, some flabby persons who are not boxers of any kind.

Now let us attempt to contrapose an I-form proposition.

| | | |
|---|---|---|
| Original: | 1. | Some novelists are conservative. |
| Obverse of 1: | 2. | Some novelists are not non-conservative. |

Converse of 2:

We cannot convert the O-form proposition as was noted in an earlier chapter, and therefore, we are stymied in our attempt to form the contrapositive of "Some novelists are conservative." If we attempt to contrapose this directly the result would be, "Some non-conservative persons are non-novelists." This happens to be true, but it follows not from the initial proposition, but from our observation of novelists. Contrapose "Some citizens are non-senators," which is true, and the result is "Some senators are non-citizens," which we would not accept as true.

### EXERCISES: CHAPTER 12

Assuming the truth of the first proposition in each of the groups of propositions numbered 1 through 14, are the propositions that follow true, false, or doubtful?

1. No one likes to have a gesture of friendship spurned.
   a. Some persons do not like to have a gesture of friendship spurned.
   b. Some persons like to have a gesture of friendship spurned.
   c. Everyone likes to have his or her gesture of friendship spurned.
   d. A few individuals like to have a gesture of friendship spurned.

    e. Everyone dislikes having a gesture of friendship spurned.

2. Some beverages are not healthful in hot weather.
   a. No beverages are healthful in hot weather.
   b. Some foods not in beverage form are healthful in in hot weather.
   c. Some things that are healthful in hot weather are not beverages.
   d. All beverages are healthful in hot weather.
   e. Some beverages are healthful in hot weather.

3. Some medical doctors are not surgeons.
   a. Some surgeons are not medical doctors.
   b. Some medical doctors are non-surgeons.
   c. Some non-medical doctors are surgeons.
   d. Some who are not surgeons are medical doctors.
   e. No surgeons are medical doctors.

4. Some ministers are witty.
   a. All ministers are witty.
   b. No ministers are witty.
   c. Some who are witty are parishioners.
   d. Those who are not ministers are witty.
   e. Some ministers are not witty.

5. All politicians like applause.
   a. Some politicians do not like applause.
   b. Some politicians like applause.
   c. No politicians like applause.
   d. No politicians like an audience that does not respond with applause.
   e. All who like applause are politicians.

6. No loitering allowed.
   a. Only loitering is not allowed.
   b. Some loitering is not allowed.
   c. Some loitering is allowed.

    d. Jogging is allowed.

    e. All loitering is allowed.

7. Some bliks are not drimps.

    a. Some drimps are not bliks.

    b. Some bliks are non-drimps.

    c. All bliks are not drimps.

    d. All bliks are drimps.

    e. Some bliks are drimps.

8. Most rockclimbers are cautious.

    a. All rockclimbers are cautious.

    b. Some rockclimbers are incautious.

    c. No rockclimbers are cautious.

    d. Most who are not rockclimbers are cautious.

    e. Some rockclimbers are careless.

9. It is false that some conservatives do not advocate wiretapping.

    a. All conservatives advocate wiretapping.

    b. Some conservatives do not advocate wiretapping.

    c. Some conservatives advocate wiretapping.

    d. Only conservatives advocate wiretapping.

    e. No conservatives advocate wiretapping.

10. It is not true that all citizens are voters.

    a. No one but a voter is a citizen.

    b. Some citizens are voters.

    c. Not all citizens are voters.

    d. Some citizens are not voters.

    e. No citizens are voters.

11. It is false that some soldiers are not expendable.

    a. No soldiers are not expendable.

    b. Some soldiers are not inexpendable.

    c. Only soldiers are not expendable.

    d. All soldiers are expendable.

    e. Some who are not expendable are soldiers.

12. It is false that no dopips are fraks.
    a. All dopips are fraks.
    b. Few dopips are fraks.
    c. Some dopips are fraks.
    d. No fraks are dopips.
    e. Some dopips are not fraks.
13. It is false that some fraks are not boodids.
    a. Only boodids are fraks.
    b. Some boodids are not fraks.
    c. No fraks are boodids.
    d. Some fraks are boodids.
    e. All fraks are boodids.
14. It is false that some plastics are tough.
    a. No plastics are tough.
    b. All plastics are tough.
    c. A few plastics are tough.
    d. Few plastics are tough.
    e. Some plastics are not tough.

Convert each of the following:
15. No cynics should be elected to public office.
16. Some book club selections are not worth their price.
17. All historians are skeptics.
18. Some senators are very wealthy men.
19. Some congressional leaders are not college graduates.
20. Some inventors have been mathematically inept men.

Obvert the propositions 15-20 above.

Contrapose the propositions 15-20 above.

## COMMENTS ON EXERCISES FOR CHAPTER 12

The following is a checklist for answers to exercises 1 through 14 for this chapter. It will be followed by comments on some of the answers which may have proved perplexing.

| 1. a. T | 5. a. F | 9. a. T | 13. a. T |
|---------|---------|---------|----------|
| b. F    | b. T    | b. F    | b. D     |
| c. F    | c. F    | c. T    | c. F     |
| d. F    | d. T    | d. D    | d. T     |
| e. D    | e. D    | e. F    | e. T     |
| 2. a. D | 6. a. D | 10. a. F | 14. a. T |
| b. D    | b. T    | b. D    | b. F     |
| c. D    | c. F    | c. T    | c. F     |
| d. F    | d. D    | d. T    | d. T     |
| e. D    | e. F    | e. D    | e. T     |
| 3. a. D | 7. a. D | 11. a. T | |
| b. T    | b. T    | b. T    | |
| c. D    | c. D    | c. D    | |
| d. T    | d. F    | d. T    | |
| e. D    | e. D    | e. F    | |
| 4. a. D | 8. a. D | 12. a. D | |
| b. F    | b. D    | b. D    | |
| c. D    | c. F    | c. T    | |
| d. D    | d. D    | d. F    | |
| e. D    | e. D    | e. D    | |

1.  d. "A few individuals like to have their gesture of friendship spurned" is a vague proposition. It must be restated, "Some individuals like to have their gesture of friendship spurned." If the original proposition, "No one likes to have his gesture of friendship spurned" is true, then, of course, the clarified proposition would be false.

2.  b. This is doubtful, since the original proposition says nothing about foods not in beverage form, only beverages.

3.  c. It appears, and indeed it is the case, that this proposition is false. But, we know this to be the case from the observation that surgeons must have training as medical doctors; the falsity does not follow from the truth of the original proposition. If all that we know is

represented by the original proposition, then this inference is doubtful. A similar argument pertains to e.

4.  Propositions c and d are doubtful, because the original proposition tells us nothing about those who are not ministers.

5.  d. In form, this proposition is correct. But, there are some difficulties involved. One is something of a four-term fallacy. When we insert the wording "an audience that does not respond with applause," we have changed the original meaning. Certainly, politicians might welcome the opportunity to speak on occasions when applause would be inappropriate, for example, to a religious gathering, or at the interment of a soldier killed in battle.

Let us formulate a syllogism based upon the initial proposition:

$$\overset{1}{} \qquad\qquad \overset{2}{}$$
All politicians like audiences that applaud.
$$\overset{3}{} \qquad\qquad \overset{4}{}$$
This is an audience that does not applaud.

Four terms clearly appear. If this is the interpretation, the statement "No politicians like an audience that does not respond with applause" would be doubtful in its relationship to the initial proposition.

6.  a. This is a vague proposition requiring restatement as "All that is not allowed is loitering." There may be other activities than loitering that are not allowed: target practice, nudity, littering, etc., insofar as the original statement is concerned.

7.  a. This statement is doubtful because the original proposition, being an O-form proposition, cannot be converted.

10. If it is not true (false) that "All citizens are voters" then it must be true that "Some citizens are not voters." This, then, is the statement appearing in d. What, then, about a and c? Proposition a is vague and should be restated "All non-voters are non-citizens," or "All non-voters are excluded from citizens." The truth of d would then render a false. Proposition c must be restated "Some citizens are not voters," and that is the wording of d, already established as true.

12. If it is false that no dopips are fraks, then it must be true that some dopips are fraks, and that is what is said in c. This, in turn, would render a and b doubtful, d false, and e doubtful.

13. a. is a vague proposition which must be stated "All fraks are boodids." If it is false that some fraks are not boodids it must be true that all fraks are boodids. This makes e true, b doubtful, c false, and d true.

14. d. must be restated as "Some plastics are not tough." If it is false that some plastics are tough then it must be true that *all* plastics are not tough, or no plastics are tough. The truth of a, then, renders b and c false and d and e true.

The converse forms of statements 15 through 20 are as follows:

15. No one should be elected to public office who is a cynic.

16. This is an O-form proposition and therefore cannot be converted.

17. Some skeptics are historians.

18. Some very wealthy men are senators.

19. This is an O-form proposition and cannot be converted.

20. Some mathematically inept men have been inventors.

The obverse forms of statements 15 through 20 are as follows:

15. All who are cynics should be non-elected to public office.
16. Some book club selections are not-worth their price.
17. No historians are non-skeptics.
18. Some senators are not non-very wealthy men.
19. Some congressional leaders are non-college graduates.
20. Some inventors have not been non-mathematically inept men.

The contraposed forms of statements 15 through 20 are as follows:

15. This must be contraposed by limitation. "Some who should not be elected to public office are not non-cynics."
16. Some books that are not worth their price are not non-book club selections.
17. All non-skeptics are non-historians.
18. This is an I-form proposition and a contraposition would be invalid.
19. Some non-college graduates are not non-congressional leaders.
20. This is an I-form proposition and cannot be contraposed.

# Chapter 13

# The Sorites and the Enthymeme

## 1. IN CATEGORICAL SYLLOGISMS

It would be convenient if arguments or lines of reasoning were always presented in neat, formal, syllogistic packaging. But, a syllogism in standard form rarely appears in an editorial or political speech or in any of the many types of discourse where it is actually most needed. Writers and speakers avoid formal syllogistic presentations, perhaps because it is difficult to make a steady flow of syllogisms interesting and attractive. Their lines of thought imply syllogisms, of course, and sometimes they imply several syllogisms at one time by linking more than three propositions and therefore more than three terms in a sequence designed as a supporting argument for a final assertion or declaration. They also often omit phrasing that would supply propositions if we were restating their views in strict logical form.

a. *Sorites*

When we encounter a series of propositions where the acceptance of one implies another, and the acceptance of the second implies still another, and so on, we have encountered a *sorites*.

The term *sorites* derives from the Greek word *soros* meaning "pile," for we face a pile of propositions. For example:

> All A's are B's.
> All B's are C's.
> All C's are D's.
> All D's are E's.
> Therefore all A's are E's.

The argument is valid. Extend Euler's circles into a series representing these terms and their relationships, and the result is a diagram like the one on this page demonstrating the validity of this sorites.

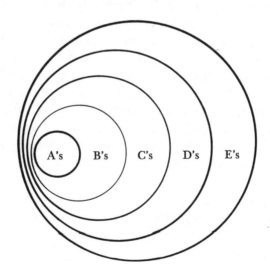

A sorites in verbal form would go something like this.

All who seek world peace are concerned about the conditions in underdeveloped countries.

All who are concerned about conditions in underdeveloped countries need to understand world economics.

All who need to understand world economics should study the works of economists representing a broad spectrum of economic theory.

All who would study the works of economists representing a broad spectrum of economic theory must spend long hours in a well stocked library.

Therefore all who seek world peace must spend long hours in a well stocked library.

However discouraging the prospect this sorites presents, it is valid and not easy to dispute as to the truth of any of the propositions involved.

If this sorites were expanded into full syllogistic form, it would appear thus:

> d S M
> Seek world peace < concerned about conditions.
> d M P
> Concerned about conditions < need economic und.
> d S P
> Therefore seek world peace < need economic und.

The second syllogism would be stated:

> d M P
> Need economic und. < study economists.
> d S M
> Seek world peace < need economic und.

<pre>
        d S                      P
</pre>
Therefore seek world peace < study economists.

The third syllogism would be stated:

<pre>
        d M                    P
</pre>
Study economists < study in library.
<pre>
        d S                    M
</pre>
Seek world peace < study economists.
<pre>
        d S                    P
</pre>
Seek world peace < study in library.

Each syllogism is valid, and so, therefore, is the sorites in its development. Note, in the expanded form, that the subject term of the first proposition in the sorites becomes the subject, or minor, term throughout. The other terms are serially replaced.

The validity of many soritical arguments is obvious at a glance. This is true of the illustration given of the need for one concerned about world peace to apply himself to study in the library. Suppose, however, that someone tries to persuade us that philosophers have no place in politics and argues, "No politician can be completely honest, for all honest people are thoroughgoing idealists. Idealists are philosophers, and, therefore, philosophers have to be excluded from the category of politicians."

There is a tangle of ambiguity here, and also a breach of a firm syllogistic rule. Our speaker seems to be implying that idealism in the sense of commitment to high ethical and esthetic goals is similar to or identical with idealism as a metaphysical view that reality is non-material in its nature. In one of the early syllogisms, then, we would encounter a four-term fallacy produced by equivocation.

Writing the propositions out in simplified form without troubling to develop each syllogism in detail would indicate an illicit minor in the making.

$$\overset{d}{\text{Politicians}} \nless \overset{d}{\text{honest.}}$$

$$\overset{d}{\text{Honest}} < \text{idealists.}$$

$$\overset{d}{\text{Idealists}} < \text{philosophers.}$$

$$\overset{d}{\text{Philosophers}} \nless \overset{d}{\text{politicians.}}$$

Note that in the third proposition, the subject term is distributed, while in the one just above it, the term is undistributed; and in the fourth proposition, the subject term is distributed, while it is not distributed in the preceding proposition.

b. *Enthymemes*

An enthymeme is an abbreviated syllogism in which one of the propositions (major premise, minor premise, or conclusion) is left unstated. The reader or listener is expected to supply the missing proposition. The name for this type of presentation derives from the Greek words *en* meaning in, and *thymos,* meaning mind, suggesting that the reader or hearer has the missing proposition in mind and will supply it automatically. An enthymeme therefore takes a form like the following:

| | | |
|---|---|---|
| (Major omitted) | $\overset{d}{M} \overset{d}{\nless} P$ | $\overset{d}{M} \overset{d}{\nless} P$ |
| $S < M$ | (Minor omitted) | $S < M$ |
| $\overset{d}{S} \overset{d}{\nless} P$ | $\overset{d}{S} \nless P$ | (Conclusion omitted) |

As has been suggested earlier, a newspaper, book, or speech written only in standard syllogistic form would be odd indeed. Imagine a political candidate saying, "All tax loopholes are included in things that should be eliminated. Tax-sheltered annuities are included in things that are tax loopholes. Therefore, tax-sheltered annuities are included

in things that should be eliminated," and following this
with syllogism after syllogism. Aside from whether it is
politically expedient to challenge tax-sheltered annuities,
such a coolly logical person would either lull his audience
to sleep or weary them with logic exercises.

An effective speaker will often delineate his argument
very carefully in private, but then rephrase it so that it will
be attractive to listen to or to read. An editorialist may
have reasoned this way in preparing his column:

> All manmade problems can be solved by man.
> The energy crisis is a manmade problem.
> Therefore the energy crisis can be solved by man.

But what the editor wrote was this:

> The energy crisis, being manmade, can be mansolved.

Another easily completed and validated enthymeme is
this one:

> All great inventors are highly imaginative and, therefore,
> find routine details boring.

The missing propositions are these:

> All who are highly imaginative find routine details boring.
> All great inventors find routine details boring.

At times when very important issues are involved, one
may be caught off guard. Following World War II, a rather
conservative senator who was concerned about more
adequate housing for veterans cosponsored a bill to provide
housing for them. An editor caused quite a stir among the
senator's constituents when he raised the question, "Has
Our Tom gone soft on communism?" Such a question involves an enthymeme. Distressed conservatives throughout
the nation handled the enthymeme very carelessly. Their
thinking seemed to follow lines represented in this
syllogism:

       d              M
Communists $<$ believe in public housing.
      d S          M
Our Tom $<$ believes in public housing.
        d S              P
Therefore Our Tom $<$ those soft on communism.

There are two conspicuous fallacies in this syllogism. The middle term has not been distributed, and the four-term fallacy has been committed. Notice that there is no P above the subject term of the major premise, for "communists" and "those soft on communism" are different terms. The term "believe in public housing" is used in two different senses. Communists believe in public ownership of all housing by definition, if not in actual practice. Senator Tom was advocating public housing for a special group, veterans, not, by any means, for everyone. Furthermore, he proposed that the financing by the federal government should be arranged so as to be advantageous to banks and realtors, so that the government would not own, except in the broadest construction of that word, any of the housing.

Such enthymemes as the following deserve careful scrutiny. "You are very apt in mathematics, so you should become a research physicist." "Professional athletics is where the big, quick money is. Son, get with that basketball!" "The United States has now limited grain sales to Russia. She must be having a hard time with Russia at the conference table." "Firm action against Japan at the time of the Manchurian invasion would have halted the Japanese warlords, prevented Mussolini from attacking little Ethiopia, and, consequently, prevented Hitler from invading Austria."

## 2. In Hypothetical Syllogisms

Sorites and enthymemes have so far been defined and

discussed in connection with the categorical syllogism. Of course, both may also be involved in hypothetical syllogisms.

### a. *Sorites*

Several "if . . . then . . ." propositions may be linked in sequential form thus:

> If A then B.
> If B then C.
> If C then D.
> If D then E.
> Therefore if A then E.

There were a good many who pondered the considerable number of democratic presidential candidates in 1975 and 1976, reasoning along a line like this: "If the Democrats do not unite early behind one of their many presidential candidates, there will be bitter fighting in primary elections. If there is bitter fighting in the primaries, Democrats will find themselves in a deadlocked convention. If the convention is deadlocked, they may nominate a compromise candidate about whom few are enthusiastic. If this turns out to be the case, they will stand to lose in the presidential election."

The Republicans had their worries, too, which were often linked up in sequence. "If President Ford continues to appear frequently in crowds, he will alienate those who have counseled caution and also those who think he is engaging too vigorously in politics when he should be tending the store. If this happens, Reagan's hand will be strengthened in broader and broader circles. If Reagan gathers much more strength, the Republican party may become divided. And, goodness knows, after Watergate, the Republican party needs a unifying and not a divisive force."

We do not need to reconstruct either sorites in detail to show that the two series of syllogisms are valid. In the hypothetical form, the minor premise needs only to con-form to the proper rule in each syllogism in the series for the sorites to have validity. The conclusion in each would serve in turn as the major premise in the succeeding syllogism. To deny the antecedent or affirm the consequent at any step would invalidate the sorites.

b. *Enthymemes*

The use of an enthymeme in an hypothetical syllogism is illustrated in the following. When a chairman of a labor union says, "As a member of this union, Jed has a right to speak on this issue," the suppressed or omitted phrasing may be put in either categorical form or hypothetical form. In the categorical form it would appear thus:

> All members of this union may speak on this issue.
> Jed is a member of this union.
> Therefore Jed may speak on this issue.

Or, one might use hypothetical phrasing.

> If one is a member of this union he has a right to speak
>   on this issue.
> Jed is a member of this union.
> Therefore Jed may speak on this issue.

Actually, it is worth noting, an enthymeme such as this often carries more psychological impact than a full, strictly logical phrasing, whether categorical or hypothetical in form. It was Aristotle's position that whenever men attempt to persuade effectively through proofs, they do so either through examples or enthymemes. "They use," he said, "nothing else."

### Exercises: Chapter 13

Test the following for validity, and comment upon their reliability. Where appropriate, supply missing propositions. In the first group S, P and M are conventionally used. The positions of missing propositions in exercise 1 are indicated by ellipses (three spaced periods).

1.  a.  . . .
    Some M is not S.
    Therefore some S is P.

    b.  . . .
    No S is M.
    Therefore some S is P.

    c.  No M is P.
    All S is M.
    Therefore . . .

    d.  . . .
    Some M is S.
    Therefore Some S is not P.

    e.  All P is M.
    Some M is S.
    Therefore  . . .

    f.  Some P is M.
    . . .
    Therefore some S is P.

g. All S is M.
   All P is M.
   Therefore . . .

h. All M is P.

   . . .

   Therefore no S is P.

i. . . .
   All M is S.
   Therefore some S is P.

j. Some M is not P.

   . . .

   Therefore, some S is not P.

2. Some misfortunes strengthen one's will. Anything that strengthens one's will is good for one. Some experiences that strengthen one's will give satisfaction. So some things that give satisfaction are good for one, including misfortunes.

3. An economist was speaking on behalf of legislation that would regulate multinational corporations. A reporter asked, "Would this mean regulating the ten leading oil companies and the six major auto manufacturers as well as the pharmaceutical concerns you have mentioned?" The candidate asked, "Do the companies you mention have at least three branches in different nations?" "So I am informed," said the reporter. "Then there's your answer," retorted the candidate.

4. All human beings deserve to be treated humanely as persons, so all criminals deserve to be treated humanely.

5. No great classical symphonies will ever completely

lose their appeal. Beethoven's symphonies will never completely lose their appeal.

6. "Yond Cassius hath a lean and hungry look. Such men are dangerous."
Shakespeare, *Julius Caesar,* act i, sc. 2.

7. "If ye were Abraham's children, ye would do the works of Abraham."
John viii. 39.

8. "He that is of God heareth God's words. Ye therefore hear them not."
John viii. 47.

9. A successful author must be either very industrious or very talented, and Agatha Christie was very industrious, as the numerous works she turned out show.

10. If Dorman's Pills are good for you, they will improve your health, and I notice that Walt, who has been taking them, has improved in health.

### COMMENTS ON EXERCISES FOR CHAPTER 13

1. a. Any premise supplied would result in the fallacy of the odd negative. A syllogism may have two negatives but one must be in the conclusion.
   b. See above.
   c. "Therefore no S is P."
   d. No M is P or no P is M, each of these forms being the converse of the other.
   e. Since M is undistributed, we cannot add a valid conclusion.
   f. The minor premise would be "All M is S."
   g. No conclusion is possible, because the middle term is undistributed.
   h. The fallacy of illicit distribution of the major term is immediately apparent here.
   i. The major premise would be either "Some P is M" or "Some M is P." The premise could be "All

P is M" or "All M is P" except for the reservation, noted earlier and explained in the appendix, about deducing an I-form proposition from two A-form propositions.

j.  The minor premise would be "All M is S." This cannot be applied in a converted form, "Some S is M," for that would result in the fallacy of the undistributed middle.

2.  This sorites would be valid except for the addition of "including misfortunes" in the conclusion. Placing the sorites in categorical form, or illustrating it with a series of circles, will reveal that "misfortunes" and "things that give satisfaction" do not necessarily overlap.

3.  The missing premise is, "All corporations having branches in three or more countries should be subject to the regulations proposed."

4.  The missing premise: "All criminals are human beings."

5.  The missing premise: "Beethoven's symphonies are great classical symphonies."

6.  The missing conclusion: "Cassius is dangerous."

7.  The missing premise, supplied in a subsequent verse, is, "Ye do not do the works of Abraham" and the missing conclusion is, "So ye are not Abraham's children." Valid.

8.  The missing premise: "For ye are not of God." Placed in hypothetical form, this would reveal the fallacy of denying the antecedent. Placed in categorical form, this would reveal the fallacy of illicit distribution of the major term.

9.  This is an instance of weak alternation, and therefore, no conclusion can be stated.

10. No conclusion is possible, for the consequent has been affirmed.

# Appendix 1

# Assisting Blind Students

## 1. The Use of Braille in Handling Informal Fallacies

Any course in which objective tests or tests requiring brief answers are suitable can be handled much more efficiently with blind students if an instructor will spend from thirty to forty-five minutes learning to read the braille alphabet by sight. This modest chore will pay off handsomely if an instructor encounters even one braillist student, and the dividends in efficiency increase with the number of braillists in a class.

The effort will also be rewarding in the personal interest one is sure to find in the ingenuity of the nineteenth century Frenchman and blind teacher of the blind, Louis Braille, who invented the remarkable system that bears his name. Braille opened up the broad vistas of the printed word to countless persons whose visual handicaps were complete or virtually so.

Braille lettering is an embossing process. It substitutes small, raised dots for printed letters. While a blind person reads these combinations of dots by touch, a sighted person can read them quite easily by sight. The reason a sighted teacher of the blind in logic and certain other courses will find it helpful to learn the braille alphabet and a few other symbols is so that students can respond to exercises, either in class or while listening to tapes, with a braille slate or with a braille typewriter, economizing considerably in time.

Consider the application in this book. The first portion of the work deals with a number of material or informal fallacies. All of these fallacies have conventionalized names: the *post hoc* fallacy (after this therefore because of this), the *ad baculum* fallacy (the appeal to force), the misuse of authority, etc. A student can listen to exercises based upon these fallacies, either in class or on tapes, or read them in braille, and respond to them in braille as quickly as sighted students can in ordinary script. He can use abbreviations in braille: P. H. for *post hoc;* A. B., or even *Ad bac.* (which is short enough to read at a glance in braille), for *ad baculum;* M. A. or Mis. Auth., for misuse of authority; and so on. An instructor can check the exercises presented in this form much more quickly than he can schedule an individual conference to test a student, listen to the student on a tape, or whatever he would otherwise do in working with an individual blind student. Even if a student forgets, for the moment, the technical name for a fallacy, he can write out the nature of the fallacy in Grade I braille, the elementary form of braille, which the instructor can read with very little loss of time.

In the second part of the book, the chapters deal with various forms of the syllogism. Certain braille symbols are assigned here, after having been tested successfully in classes with blind students, to indicate technical matters like inclusion, exclusion, distribution of terms, identification of terms, "if ... then," "either ... or" and other items. This enables the blind student to work efficiently with syllogistic processes by rewriting syllogisms in shortened form.

## 2. Learning the Braille Alphabet

The braille cell is composed of six dots arranged and numbered thus:

```
1  ● ●  4
2· ● ●  5
3  ● ●  6
```

Braillists often have occasion to refer to the letters by calling them dot 1 for "a," dots 1, 2 for "b," and on through to dots 1, 5, 3 for "o," and dots 1, 3, 5, 6 for "z."

The braille alphabet is presented below divided into three lines. It is usually advised that one learn these line by line, first a through j, then k through t, and then u through z, or, in this case, through w. When Louis Braille devised his system "w" was seldom used in French. The letter "w" was adapted when braille came into usage in English.

| a | b | c | d | e | f | g | h | i | j |
|---|---|---|---|---|---|---|---|---|---|

| k | l | m | n | o | p | q | r | s | t |
|---|---|---|---|---|---|---|---|---|---|

| u | v | x | y | z | w |
|---|---|---|---|---|---|

Note first the letters a through j. They are all formed in the upper two-thirds of the cell. Single out for the moment the letters d, f, h and j. With the exception of d, these look like a portion of the letters the dots represent. And, one who happens to have a bit of acquaintance with Hebrew will note the similarity of d and the shape of the fourth letter of the Hebrew alphabet, "daleth." The letters a, b, and c can be remembered from almost a glance. The letters e and i are unforgettable once it is noted they slant in opposite directions in the cell.

In line two, notice that k through t are formed merely by adding dot 3 to each of the letters in the first line.

Line three then adds dot 6 to the first five letters in line two, or, if you prefer, dots 3 and 6 to the first five letters in line one. That leaves only w, which, as a special case, leaves an indelible print in the memory.

A few minutes practice making pencil dots on paper helps. At first try, run through each line until you have mastered it. Then, write out, or rather dot out, the alphabet. Then, scramble letters and check back with the alphabet for accuracy.

Since students who use braille automatically use numbers, capital letter signs, and punctuation, an instructor will find some of these appearing in sets of exercises. For convenience, then, the reference list is given below. The patterns are such that they can be memorized even more quickly than the alphabet.

*Braille Numbers*

Braille numbers are formed by a number sign, dots 3, 4, 5, 6, preceding a for one, preceding b for two and so on.

*Braille Capital Sign*

Dot 6 in the cell preceding a letter indicates the letter is capitalized. Capital d:      Capital t:

*Braille Period*

The braille period consists of dots 2, 5, 6 and it looks like the letter d dropped into the lower dots in the cell:

This covers about all one encounters in the first portion of this text in the way of braille usage. However, one may pursue a fascinating study by securing (at nominal cost) Leland Schubert's *Handbook for Learning to Read Braille by Sight* from the American Printing House for the Blind, Louisville, Kentucky.

As one gets into this area of study, more opportunities open up even beyond the teaching field. For example, sighted braillists are now being sought for research on what is psychologically involved in learning to read efficiently. What, psychologists want to know, are the differences in memory storage involved in tactile reading as compared with visual reading? The University of North Carolina's Psychometric Center is initiating this and other kinds of related studies.

The following is a list of abbreviations which either sighted or visually handicapped students may use in responding to exercises in the first six chapters of this text.

| FALLACY | SUGGESTED ABBREVIATION |
|---|---|
| *Chapter* 1 | |
| 1. Equivocation | Eq, or Equiv |
|   a. Simple Ambiguity | SA, or S Amb |
|   b. Amphiboly | Amph |
| 2. Euphemism | Eu |
| 3. Obscuration | Obs |
| 4. Accent, or Lifting Out of Context | Acc, or LOC |
| 5. Leading Questions, or Complex Questions | LQ, or CQ |
| 6. Errors in Conversion | Conv |
| 7. Errors in Obversion | Obv |
| *Chapter* 2 | |
| 1. Extension | Ext |
| 2. Misuse of Humor | MH |
| 3. Appeal to Ignorance, or *Argumentum ad Ignorantiam* | AI, or Ad Ign |
| 4. Appeal to Force, or *Argumentum ad Baculum* | AF, or Ad Bac |
| 5. Appeal Against the Man or *Argumentum ad Hominem*, or Genetic Fallacy, or *Tu Quoque* | AAM, or ad Hom, or GF, or TQ |
| 6. Pettifogging, or Nit-picking | Pet, or Nit |
| *Chapter* 3 | |
| 1. Accident, or the Fallacy of the General Rule | Acdt, or FGR |

FALLACY                          SUGGESTED ABBREVIATION

2. Converse Accident, or Hasty
      Generalization              CA, or HG
3. Composition                   C, or Comp
4. Division                      D, or Div
5. *Post Hoc*                    PH
6. Special Pleading              SP
7. Oversimplification            O Simp, or Simp
8. Black-or-White                BW
9. Argument of the Beard         AB, or Beard

*Chapter* 4
1. Misuse of Authority, or
      *Argumentum ad Verecundiam*   MA, or ad Ver
2. Dogmatic Manner               Dog
3. Aphorism Citing, or Cliché
      Usage                      AC, or CU
4. Rationalization               Rat

*Chapter* 5
1. Misuse of Analogy             M Anal
2. Internal Inconsistencies, or
      Contradictory Terms        II, or CT
3. Hypothesis Contrary to Fact   HCF
4. Begging the Question, or
      Circular Reasoning, or
      Petitio Principii          BQ, CR, or PP
5. Well Poisoning                WP

*Chapter* 6
1. Emotional Language            EL, or Emot
2. Appeal to Misery, or
      *Argumentum ad
      Misericordiam*             AM, or ad Mis
3. Appeal to Special Tastes      AST, or Sp T
4. Appeal to Popular Tastes, or
      *Argumentum ad Populum*    APT, or Ad Pop


An instructor may wish to prepare exercises to supplement those at the ends of chapters, tests and examinations in braille.

He may do this himself by securing a braille font for an IBM Selectric typewriter (keyboard chart and directions for use included) from Camwil, Incorporated, 835 Keeaumoko Street, Honolulu, Hawaii 96814. This is more practical for the person who wishes to develop considerable facility in the use of braille than for those who expect to have rather limited use for braille. The keyboard chart is ingeniusly worked out, but it leads one into an advanced grade of Braille. For example, in lieu of capital letters, which are not needed, there being a conventional braille symbol placed before a letter to indicate upper case or capitalization, the chart has over the "a" an "ea," over the "s" a "wh," over the "d" a "dis," over the "f" a "to," and so on, through a number of shorthand-like symbols.

For most instructors, it is recommended that they plan their work ahead so that they may have the materials put into braille by professionals. The National Braille Association, Inc., 85 Godwin Avenue, Midland Park, New Jersey 07432, will reproduce materials in Braille very inexpensively. This association was of great help in preparing materials used in the courses from which this text issued.

### 3. THE USE OF BRAILLE WITH SYLLOGISMS, EULER'S CIRCLES AND VENN DIAGRAMS

a. *The Categorical Syllogism*

In reducing categorical propositions and syllogisms to a shortened form, as recommended in the early part of Chapter 7, braillist students have found the following procedures helpful. Just as the sighted student should rewrite the terms of a syllogism in abbreviated form and leave space for the later insertion of symbols (S for minor term, P for major term, M for middle term, d for distribution, the sidewise V and slashed sidewise V for inclusion and exclusion), so must the blind student using a braille slate leave room for the insertion of the various symbols.

A student may use either of two procedures, whichever he finds the more convenient and comfortable. First, he may leave a row of cell spaces above each proposition in the syllogism and return to that space to insert the appropriate symbols. Or, second, he may leave four cell spaces at the left of the first term of a proposition and seven cell spaces between the two terms of the proposition.

The symbols for distribution and for the terms of propositions are conventional letters and so pose no problem. But what can be done about symbols for inclusion and exclusion? A blind student proposed that dots 2, 4, 6 ⠱ be used for inclusion since, if lines connected these dots, the figure would resemble the conventional sidewise V for inclusion. This can be recognized at a glance even by the teacher in the amateur stage of work with braille. But then what can be done about the slashed sidewise V which indicates exclusion? The student suggested, "Use the letter o, dots 1, 5, 3 ⠅ , the reverse of dots 2, 4, 6, for exclusion. How often would one examining the kinds of propositions the logician deals with encounter an 'o' in the middle of a proposition? I would say never." So this convention was adopted too.

Dean Hutcheson prefers dots 2, 6, or the braille plus sign, for inclusion and dots 4, 5, 6 followed by dots 2, 6 for the slash plus sign, since dots 2, 4, 6 and 1, 3, 5 are used in mathematical braille for round brackets. Again it might be noted that dots 2, 4, 6 or dots 1, 3, 5 standing alone in the body of a proposition would cue the student in on inclusion or exclusion rather than a bracket symbol.

b. *The Hypothetical Syllogism*

Dots 1, 3, 4, 5, 6 ⠽ which form the braille letter "y" may be used for the horseshoe in the hypothetical syllogism when abbreviated by inserting it between the terms of the major proposition, always following the antecedent. These dots if connected would resemble a squared horseshoe symbol and a "y" is very easy to remember and recognize as a symbol for "if . . . then" or the sign of implication.

For the "If and only if" form of the proposition the "y"

may be repeated. "If and only if you fulfill the terms of the contract will you be paid in full" would appear thus in abbreviated form:

Fulfill ⠿ ⠿ paid

The braille using student would, of course, put the terms in braille also.

Dean Hutcheson offers an alternative for the hypothetical proposition. He has used the braille question mark, dots 2, 3, 6, for the horseshoe symbol and the braille dash, dots 3, 6 followed by dots 3, 6 for "if and only if" propositions.

## c. *Alternation and Disjunction*

Since a single V represents "Either ... or ... or both"—simple alternation—and a double V represents "Either ... or ... but not both"—strong alternation (the combination of alternation with disjunction) the braille representations of these prove suitable for abbreviating the major propositions in syllogisms inolving alternation. Certainly one does not expect to find a V or a VV in any but a specialized usage such as this.

The simple disjunction is sufficiently rarely met that the braillist student perhaps just as well use the dash followed by parentheses enclosing the term, dot and term—the conventional arrangement to indicate disjunction.

## d. *The Dilemma.*

Symbols for use with the dilemma are those discussed in relation to the hypothetical, alternative and disjunctive syllogisms, of course.

An instructor accustomed to J. Lukasiewicz' Polish system of notation may prefer to use it with braille using students. In some respects it would be simpler for such students. The following columns show the Polish system on the left, notations used in this text in the center and their verbalized form on the right.

| Np | $-p$ | not p |
| Kpq | $p.q$ | both p and q |
| Cpq | $p \supset q$ | if p then q |
| Epq | $p \supset \supset q$ | p if and only if q |
| Apq | $pVq$ | either p or q or both |
| Jpq | $pVVq$ | either p or q but not both |

The Polish system is efficient when one prefers working with formulas. The system adapted for use in this text is the one to which the author first became accustomed. Moreover it appears to him that the system has certain advantages for the beginning student. The symbols are easy to learn, some of them are familiar, and they seem to keep the meaning of propositions being examined a bit more clearly in the thinking of the student thus commanding to that degree attention and interest.

### e. *Euler's Circles*

The student who has a serious visual handicap poses a problem for the instructor who uses Euler's Circles and Venn Diagrams. But this problem can be easily resolved. For Euler's Circles simply cut out of light but sturdy plastic three discs—one an inch in diameter, a second two inches in diameter, and a third three inches in diameter. Be sure the edges are smooth. Braillists seem to develop sensitive fingers and a fingertip scratched by a rough bit of plastic could prove discommoding.

The student can handle these discs while listening to the instructor or tapes explaining the representation of terms of a syllogism. In the doleful syllogism about the mortality of men and of Socrates, students are instructed to let the large circle or disc represent "mortal things," the next larger circle represent "all men," being placed within the largest circle, and the smaller circle—Socrates—being placed within the second circle. The student will readily discern by his touch that if the small circle, Socrates, is within the circle representing all men and that circle is within a still larger circle representing mortal beings, then Socrates is bound to be inside the larger circle of mortal beings.

The blind student who finds, as the sighted student often will also, that a syllogism does not give clear directions as to where one of the circles must go will know that he has encountered an argument or syllogism that is not valid.

Another way of handling Euler's Circles with the blind student enables him to discuss the categorical syllogism before the class—to do a form of board work. This calls for a rubberized blackboard with the kinds of tacks used for such boards and three discs cut from pasteboard or a manila folder. It is helpful to make these discs large enough for the class to see them easily and it is further helpful for them to be painted distinctly different colors. The student can illustrate the positioning of terms of a syllogism with these items very easily. The blind students in the research groups associated with this study used a large beige disc cut from a manila folder, a slightly smaller disc from the same material and colored red, and a third still smaller disc colored black.

A similar procedure utilizes metal boards with Euler's Circles attached to magnets. In this case some open space needs to be left in cutting out the discs so that the magnets will not dislodge too easily because of accumulated thicknesses of material between them and the metal board.

### f. *Venn Diagrams*

For Venn Diagrams an embossed design mounted on plastic is useful. A fairly heavy grade of aluminum foil about five inches square can be embossed with a braille stylus or with the tip of a ball point pen. Blind students prefer that the labels for the diagrams be embossed in braille rather than in printed letters and numbers. As in preparing plastic discs to represent Euler's Circles care must be exercised to see that the aluminum foil is not cut through leaving any sharp points or edges. In mounting the design on plastic the grooves are filled with glue as the aluminum is glued to a piece of sturdy plastic. The hardened supporting glue produces a symbol that is very durable and will withstand considerable accidental abuse.

The following compares the use of Venn Diagrams by

sighted and visually handicapped students. The sighted student shades out excluded sections while the blind student uses rectangular plastic counters to cover excluded areas. As an illustration let us use the following:

    dM             P
All dogs are mammals.
      d S                M
All miniature dachshunds are dogs.
      d S                P
Therefore all miniature dachshunds are mammals.

An even more convenient and precise device for utilizing the Venn Diagrams employs the principles of a braille chessboard or checkerboard as suggested by Professor Walhout. Suppliers of educational materials can provide a form of easily carved plywood. From this wood there are carved to a consistent depth the inner portions of the three overlapping circles so that only the circle lines remain raised. These are numbered with the conventional 1–7 numbers either by indented slots or raised dots using small drops of glue or pinheads implanted by snapping off all but about ¼ inch of the pin.

Seven blocks are cut to fit these segments, protruding slightly above the circle lines so they can be easily inserted and removed. In diagramming, if a proposition calls for shading out 4 and 7, say, as in "All M are included in P," one simply inserts blocks 4 and 7 which fit in like checkers.

In the case of particular propositions, for example, "Some S are included in P," holes are made in each indented area for a peg to be inserted in the appropriate hole to indicate class membership. In the case of uncertain membership, for example, an X in 2 or 5 but no clarity as to which, one uses instead of the overlapping bar a two-peg device linked by a wooden bar, that is, a bar with a peg on each end that fits into both holes.

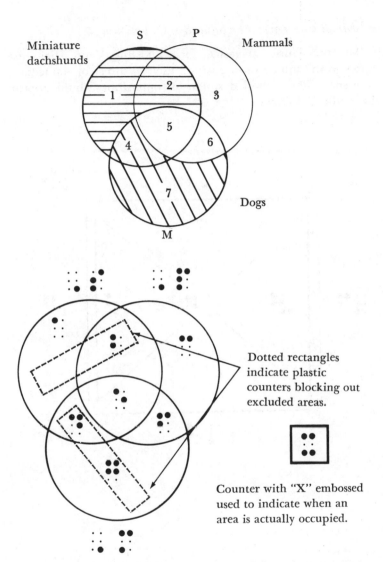

Dotted rectangles indicate plastic counters blocking out excluded areas.

Counter with "X" embossed used to indicate when an area is actually occupied.

### g. *Direct Inference: The Square of Opposition*

The procedures suggested for embossing Venn Diagrams apply to the square of opposition used in direct or immediate inference. The embossed square of opposition would appear in braille as follows:

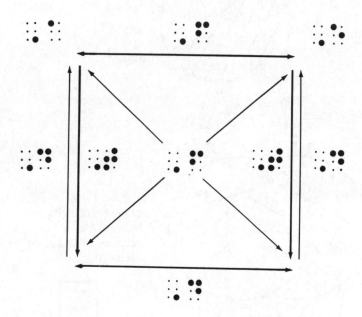

### h. *Transcribing the Text for Use by the Blind*

In transcribing a work of this type either onto tapes or into braille, it is necessary to repeat materials from time to time. The sighted student can refer to a preceding page or an earlier portion of the text rather easily, if an explanation of a point or an exercise requires it. But, a blind student will be much slower in the process of using braille, and he will be even slower if he has to search out the lines referred to by rewinding and replaying sections of tapes. The transcriber must either check out the materials before beginning a transcription, spotting points that will need to be repeated, or be attentively deliberate and careful in a first reading to note such points.

The repeating of items is especially necesary in dealing with explanations regarding exercises at the end of each chapter. The transcriber is advised, then, first of all to check a set of such exercises in both parts of the book to see the extent to which repetition will be needed.

# Appendix 2

# Causal Analysis

In connection with the discussion of the *post hoc* fallacy and the fallacy of converse accident, a presentation of causal analysis is in order. Simply because one event follows another one, it is not to be concluded on the basis of sequence alone that the first event caused the second or that the second was in any way prompted necessarily by the first. Earlier illustrations are applicable: difficulties Apollo 13 experienced after lifting off at 2:13 on a Friday the thirteenth; a dark birthmark on a child "caused" by her mother's excitement at seeing the smoke of a burning house; the probable origin of various superstitions, etc.

According to David Hume, an eighteenth century Scottish historian and philosopher, causation in and of itself cannot be empirically demonstrated, and his position is difficult to refute. Causation cannot be seen, smelled, felt, heard, or tasted. Without some notions of causation, on the other hand, we would be paralyzed. We would have no reliable notion that food would nourish. So, we would not eat. We would not know that water would quench thirst, and so, we would not drink. We would not know that fire would warm us or cook meals for us, and so, we would not light one. Debates continue over whether Hume was correct in his conclusion that the notion of causation is a result of habit building, rather than of reliable experience and analysis of that experience.

Historians have reported so many improper designations of causation that we must face the fact that establishing causal relations is often a very difficult undertaking. George Washington, it has been reported, was subjected to bloodletting and was forced to drink bourbon because he was flushed and had a high pulse rate and temperature, leading his physicians to conclude he had too much thick blood. It needed, they thought, to be reduced in amount and thinned. If, as some contemporary physicians believe from a record of his symptoms, George Washington had a streptococcic infection, he may have succumbed to that infection aggravated by quite the wrong treatment. An error had been made in the diagnosis of causation.

Quite some decades ago British sailors, who were fond of citrus fruits, were noted to be comparatively free of scurvy. They loaded their ship's larders with limes to prevent scurvy. Hence, perhaps, they came by the nickname "Limies." Lime, then, and other citrus fruits were believed to cause freedom from scurvy. Eventually, of course, it was learned that the presence of vitamin C in citrus fruits was incompatible with the presence of scurvy in those who ate citrus fruits. And so, it was the discovery of that vitamin and its synthesizing that made it no longer necessary to eat citrus fruits except for enjoyment. The ship's doctor needed only to take along a few bottles of vitamin C tablets and not barrels of fruit in order to have a scurvy-free crew.

Those who are past fifty years of age will very likely recall Saturday movie matinees when the theater was permeated with the strong and unpleasant odor of asafoetida, a resin suspended in a small cloth bag about numerous children's necks to ward off (i.e., to cause to stay away) whatever might bring the child low, be it influenza, pneumonia, or poliomyelitis.

The odor of asafoetida has not been abroad in crowded auditoriums for many a year, as one who remembers it can report with profound gratitude. Calomel, sulfur and molasses, and many other supposed preventives and remedies have gone the way of asafoetida. The revered, and often deservedly so, medical profession has so often changed its mind as to causation that one is given pause. How does one determine or identify causation? If medical doctors, who have rather circumscribed situations to consider in regard to causation, have often been puzzled or in error, then it is the case that those dealing with broad situations—agriculturists, meteorologists, economists, sociologists and others—have an even broader and more complicated problem.

In the early part of the nineteenth century, J. F. W. Herschel and John Stuart Mill presented a method that has become widely accepted as helpful in identifying causal relations to a degree of reasonable reliability. The method, in its form most frequently associated with Mill, proposed the following, some of which help singly but which must be combined in some situations.

1. The establishment of agreement. This means the necessity of spotting a factor or certain factors present in each instance of an occurrence in which a causal phenomenon is suspected.
2. The establishment of difference. This means the establishing of a factor or certain factors present with the occurrence of a seeming causal phenomenon and absent without the occurrence of such a seeming causal phenomenon.
3. The establishment of joint agreement and difference. This is combining the procedures noted under 1 and 2.
4. The establishment of concomitant variations. This is the establishing of the relevance of a factor which varies, or certain factors which vary, in either direct or inverse relationship in the sequence of events under study.
5. The consideration of residues. This requires the recording of remaining, or residual, factors beyond those mentioned in 1 through 4. The more of these steps one can apply in

the observation of phenomena thought to be involved in causal relationships, or in controlled experimentation pertaining to suspected cause-effect relationships, the better. Let us illustrate these in turn.

1. The Method of Agreement can be illustrated easily by boiling some ordinary drinking water at sea-level and registering its temperature, 100° C. Finding that a quart of the water would boil at that temperature regardless of the kind of material its container was made of, or the size of the container, or the kind of heat applied, we would conclude with a considerable degree of confidence that the heat reaching the thermometer through the water was causing it to register at 100° C.

2. The Method of Difference requires that all conditions in a situation be repeated with one item introduced and withdrawn. Thus, we learned in elementary chemistry that sodium or any of its compounds will give a bright yellow double line in spectroscopic viewing. When there is no sodium, there is no such line. When sodium is present, even in any form of compound, the yellow line appears.

3. The Joint Method of Agreement and Difference is illustrated by the unpleasant fact that it is difficult to buy cucumbers at the market which are free of a disagreeable wax substance. Shippers discovered sometime ago that a crate of waxed cucumbers and a crate of unwaxed cucumbers differed widely in their ability to reach the market unbruised and without shriveling or decay. The method of agreement would support a causal relationship between the persisting soundness of the waxed cucumbers, while the contrast between the crates would bring the method of difference into consideration.

4. The Method of Concomitant Variations has been observed by all of us in some form, even though we may not have known the traditional title for what we were observing. Anyone who has polished metals, wood, or stone has observed that rubbing produces friction and heat, and that the amount of heat produced varies rather markedly with the texture of the

material involved, the pressure placed upon the objects involved, and the vigor of the rubbing.

5. The Method of Residues could hardly be more easily illustrated than by a common method of determining the weight of coal one is getting in a truckload. Weigh the empty truck and record the weight. Fill it with coal and weigh the loaded truck. Substract the weight of the empty truck and the residue, that left over, is the weight of the coal. Or, note the familiar use of multiple lamp bulbs. If there are three 60-watt bulbs in a lamp, switch on one and note the intensity. Add another and note the intensity. Switch on the third, and one concludes that the second degree of intensity was caused by the second bulb, and the third degree of intensity is caused by the third bulb. Extinguish the third bulb and the second bulb and the lessening light indicates something about the method of residues.

Mill's methods, as clear as they are, require careful, conscientious application. They are easily abused. Take, for example, the perversion of the method of agreement in the following anecdote. Tom, Dick, Harry, and Reggie were commiserating about their hangovers following a lively party the night before. Each reported that he had stuck with one kind of drink all evening—Tom with scotch and soda, Dick with whisky and soda, Harry with rum and soda, and Reggie with vodka and soda. They pledged with one accord, "No more soda for me." This illustration, first reported as a small joke, no doubt, is applicable in that we are aware that there are other factors to be considered that would require the sustained use of Mill's whole slate of methods to get at the cause of the hangovers. The drinks contained alcohol, which one physician has aptly termed "a rough chemical." The drinks contained oils which the distillers may not have eliminated and flavorings which could conceivably be contributing factors. But to complicate the matter even further, some psychologists are contending that, except for the ingestion of such inordinate quantities of alcoholic beverages as to wreak considerable havoc on certain tissues, some hangovers have a psychological basis.

The method of difference is subject to misuse similar to that of our four tipplers, as in the case of the superstitious man who said, "I've always heard it was bad luck to open an umbrella in the house. Monday and Tuesday were good sales days. Wednesday rain was blowing hard, and so, I opened my umbrella in the hallway. I had a rotten day all around. Thursday and Friday business picked up wonderfully." For this fellow, then, opening the umbrella was the only different act of the week which could account for a poor sales day.

Even the relatively more sophisticated method of concomitant variation can be mishandled. One might make a statistical correlation between the display of the aurora borealis and the seasonal scores of one's favorite athletic team, but to conclude immediately that there is a causal relation would appear to be somewhat absurd.

One more thing about Mill's methods deserves mention. Just as his methods can be used to give inductive support to the very high probability that certain causal connections exist, so they can be used in a negative fashion to show certain causal connections highly improbable. Pliny the Elder used a principle of Mill's negatively several centuries before Mill formulated his methods. Pliny challenged astrologers something like this. "If, as you claim, the destiny of man is set by the sign of the zodiac under which he was born, then all men born at the same time under a given sign should have the same destiny. But men of widely different kinds of fortune, masters, slaves, kings, beggars, strong men and weak men, courageous men and cowards are born under the same sign. Your claim is false."

# Appendix 3

# Two Special Cases Involving Particular Propositions

## SPECIAL CASE 1

From two I-form, or particular, propositions, no conclusion is possible. Such an arrangement would involve the fallacy of the undistributed middle term. It is thus the case that when two propositions have the subject term qualified by "some," the occupied areas, if we are using circles, do not necessarily overlap. Examine the following syllogism.

Some Lakeside College students take logic.
Some Lakeside College students take ceramics.
Therefore some Lakeside College logic students also take ceramics courses.

Let a large circle represent those who take logic. Let a second circle represent students and place it so that it overlaps or intersects with the larger circle. Where would one place a third circle representing those taking ceramics? The circle could overlap only the circle representing students, without touching the circle representing those taking logic. The syllogism does not instruct us to place the circle representing ceramics students so as to overlap the circle representing logic students. Therefore the syllogism is invalid.

But, there is an interesting problem occasioned by propositions with the quantifier "most" instead of "all" or "some." "Most" is not "all" and therefore cannot be construed as quantifying an A-proposition. At the same time, some logicians are not happy with construing "most" as "some" since this makes it an I-proposition which gives it undeserved status as a proposition with "existential import," a concept we must examine next.

In any case, the situation appears to be this. When the quantifier "most" is used with the subject of both premises in a syllogism, it may be possible to derive a valid conclusion. The following syllogism is an illustration.

> Most Lakeside students take physical education.
> Most Lakeside students take English.
> Therefore some Lakeside students who take physical
>   education also take English.

The validity of this syllogism can be shown by using rectangles which are more convenient than circles in this case.

Solid line: students.
Dotted line: physical education
  students.
Dashes: English students.
"X" indicates area occupied
  by both groups.

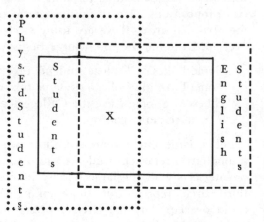

Let a large rectangle represent Lakeside students. Represent the first premise by constructing a rectangle of dots—representing physical education majors—overlapping the first rectangle. This rectangle must cover more than half the area of the first rectangle. Now construct a third rectangle of dashes—representing English students—covering more than half of the area of the first rectangle. The dotted rectangle and the rectangle drawn with dashes clearly must overlap. And so, the result must read, "Some Lakeside students take both physical education and English."

But, one must examine each individual case. The fact that a major and minor premise both begin with the word "most" does not mean they will automatically yield a valid conclusion. The quantifier "most" must appear in the middle term in both premises, the term whose business it is to link the major and minor terms. If "most" appears in a term other than the middle term, a linkage is by no means forced.

Examine the following situation in which "most" appears in the middle and minor terms.

> Most wrestlers are actors.
> Most actors are members of an actors' guild.

It is not possible to conclude that some wrestlers are, therefore, members of an actors' guild. Examine the following diagram:

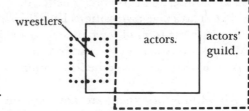

Solid line: actors.
Dotted line: wrestlers
Dashes: actors' guild.

This can also be illustrated by some simple arithmetic. Suppose we have 2,000 actors, 1,500 actors' guild members and 300 wrestlers. Since there are 500 actors who do not belong to a guild, there is ample room for most or even all of the 300 wrestlers to be among the actors who do not belong to the actors' guild.

## SPECIAL CASE 2

The second special case concerning the categorical syllogism will be of interest primarily to the student who pursues the study of logic to a higher level. From two universal propositions, a particular conclusion may not be deduced.

There are two reasons for this. First, at the basic level of study, there is no point to being content with a particular affirmative conclusion when two universal affirmative propositions would yield a universal affirmative conclusion. We would normally state a universal affirmative conclusion.

All consumers are concerned with inflation.
All housewives are consumers.

There is little point to concluding: "Some housewives are concerned with inflation." We would be inclined to assert, rather, that "all housewives are concerned with inflation," and that would be valid. Logicians, however, consider particular propositions as asserting existence. The technical expression for this is that "particular propositions have 'existential import.' "

In the basic form of logic presented in this work, commonly called Aristotelian logic, a universal affirmative proposition has an unexpressed hypothetical notion as in the following:

All whisbies (if there are any whisbies) are tiddledums (if there are any tiddledums).
All poods (if there are any poods) are whisbies (if there are any whisbies).

Therefore all poods (if there are any poods) are
tiddledums (if there are any tiddledums).

This syllogism is valid, despite the fact that at least whisbies
and tiddledums are not known to exist. ("Poods," it turns out
after this syllogism was composed, is a Russian unit of weight.)
The concern here is with the logical relationship of the terms
and not with their actual existence as something subject, say,
to sensory experience.

Since the work of the nineteenth century English mathematician George Boole, however, logicians have adopted the convention that an I-proposition declares existence. The proposition, "Some housewives are concerned about inflation," then,
would mean that there is at least one housewife who is concerned about inflation.

The reasons for such an interpretation of the I-proposition
would require more extensive discussion than is warranted in
a study limited largely to practical, day-to-day tools of reason.
So, we shall consider a couple of illustrations which suggest
the basic reason for considering the I-proposition as declaring
existence. We will do this in the hope of impressing upon the
student the need for remembering the rule involved, especially
in the event that he or she pursues the study of logic at a
more advanced level.

Remembering that *validity* in reasoning requires that a
conclusion be logically forced by the premises, and that a
*reliable* conclusion, one that is forced and true, requires that
the premises be true and so related as to force the conclusion,
consider the following:

All one-horned animals are herbivores.
All unicorns are one-horned animals.
Therefore some unicorns are herbivores.

The first two propositions, the premises, are true in the sense
that because they are hypothetical they really say, "All one-

horned animals (if there are any) are herbivores (if there are any) . And all unicorns (if there are any) are one-horned animals (if there are any) ." Or, the propositions, one of them at least, may be considered true (in a sense) by definition. So the premises are true, but the conclusion is false, because it declares that there are unicorns while unicorns do not exist. We have moved from hypothetical instances to a declaration of existence. We have forced a conclusion, but we cannot declare it true, for unicorns do not exist. We cannot define things into existence.

Or, consider a situation we might experience. A game warden at a check point near trout waters cautions us, "The limit is ten trout." We interpret this to mean, "All who catch more than the limit will be fined." This means, put another way, "If anyone catches more than the limit, he will be fined." This does not declare that any fisherman or fishermen will exceed the limit. The warning is given in the hope that no exceeders of the limit will in fact exist. Later, we return to the checkpoint and see that the warden has examined the fish caught by two fellows who apparently hoped he would be off duty. They had caught twelve trout each. Now we can say, "Some have exceeded the limit." This depicts the fact that "Some fishermen exist who have exceeded the limit." For emphasis we repeat the rule: From two universal propositions a particular conclusion may not be deduced.

# Index